RESCUE me

A unique approach to diet and exercise for weight loss

Judith Kennedy
Matthew Squires

This book is a living piece of research collecting information on the results you achieve at www.rescuemeonline.com

Oncology Children's Foundation
www.ocf.com.au

Rescue Me supports the Oncology Children's Foundation

NEW HOLLAND

Published by:
Lamp Post Holdings Pty. Limited
79 Bland Street, Ashfield, 2131, NSW, Australia
2A Stafford Street, Stanmore, 2048 NSW, Australia
E-mail: info@rescuemeonline.com
Web: www.rescuemeonline.com

© Judith Kennedy-Matthew Squires

Authors: Judith Kennedy and Matthew Squires

Publisher: Lamp Post Holdings Pty Limited
Design concepts: Matthew Squires and Judith Kennedy
Illustrations: Chris Wahl
Photographer: Oliver Strewe
Editor/Proof Reader: Sally Zwartz
Stock Photography: R&R Publishers

The National Library of Australia
Cataloguing-in-Publication Data

Title: Rescue me : A unique approach to diet and exercise for weight loss

ISBN: 9781741106848

1. Weight loss. 2. Exercise. 3. Health. 4.Physical fitness.

613.712

This edition published by:
New Holland Publishers
1/66 Gibbes Street,
Chatswood NSW 2067
Australia

All rights reserved. No part of this book may be stored, reproduced or transmitted in any form or by any means without written permission of the publishers, except in the case of brief quotations embedded in critical articles and reviews.

Printed in Singapore

Foreword

Why this book will change your life

The first time I met Judith Kennedy I was immediately aware I was in the presence of an irresistible force. As Deputy Chair of the Board of the Oncology Children's Foundation, she had driven an extraordinary growth in the capacity of the Foundation to support our childhood cancer research. She is blessed with clarity of vision and a relentless determination to deliver change for the future. Her support of our cancer research allowed us to attack major issues in childhood cancer. Your purchase of this book will further support our work and we thank you.

When Judith first explained this book to me, I was excited by her straightforward approach to this health problem. We all know the threat that is obesity in the 21st century. The hospitals are already seeing an increase in type 2 diabetes of epidemic proportions. What is truly extraordinary is the realisation that this has been caused by a failure in personal and family responsibility. Judith and Matthew Squires have confronted this issue where it belongs – with you and your family and your collective responsibilities.

My first response when I read this book was relief. It deals with the key concepts and is very, very practical. This is not a book to leave on your coffee table or untouched on a bookshelf. This book provides you with a sensible approach to deal with the key issues, exercise and healthy eating. Health is not a hard idea to get your head around. Respect your body in terms of how you exercise it and what you put into it. Not too hard to grasp the logic, but sometimes hard to take personal responsibility to make it happen.

This book is like a roadmap for taking responsibility for your future. I have seen the transformation in Judith's life. I hope that this book will do the same for you. I know it has that potential. This is the start of your future and the future is looking good. I wish you well as you move to transform the lives of you and your family and I thank you for your support of our research.

Professor Peter Gunning
Head,
Oncology Research Unit
The Children's Hospital at Westmead, Australia

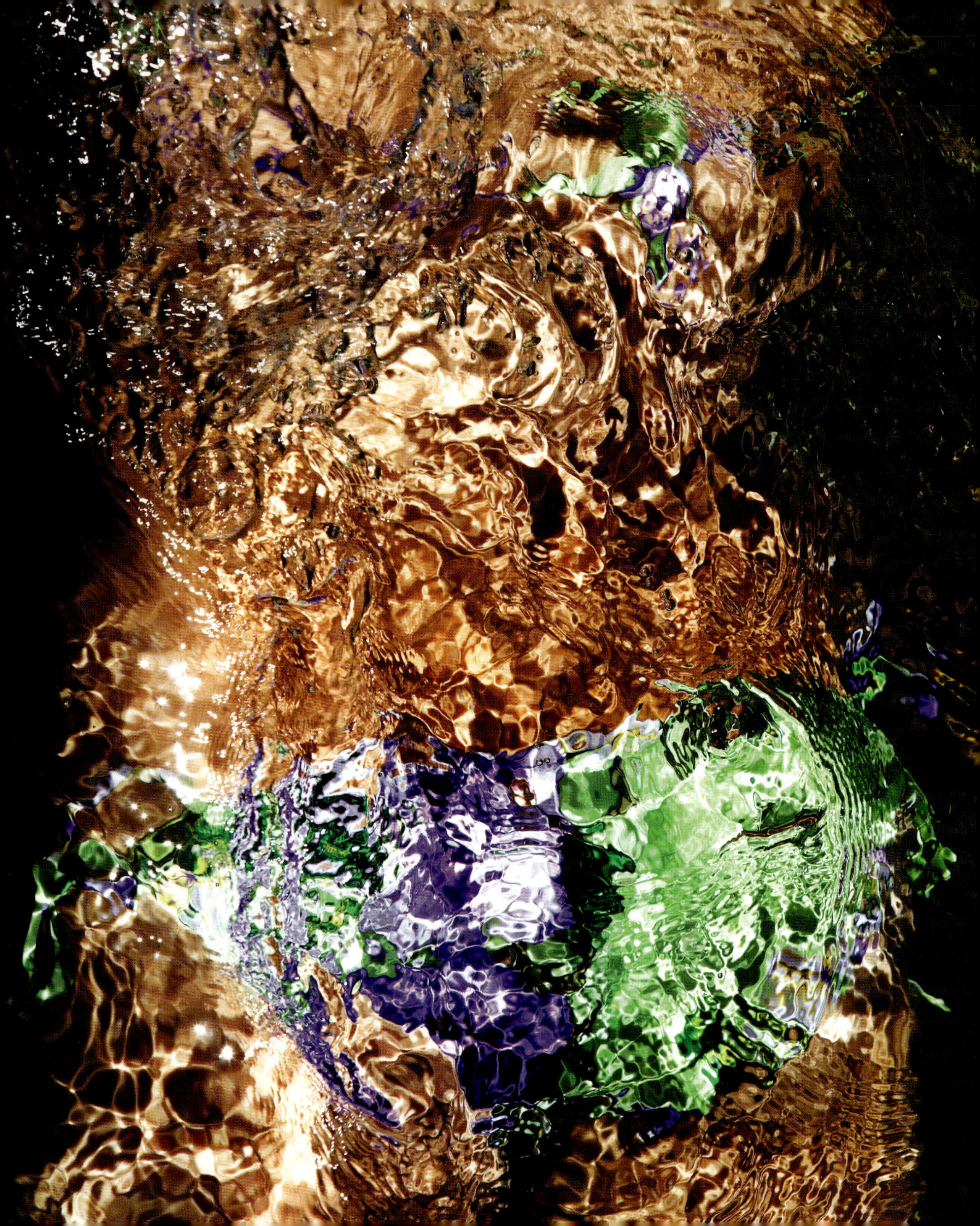

Contents

7	Chapter 1	In the raw - obesity at the heart of the problem	
		Metabolic syndrome	
17	Chapter 2	The secret to the rescue	
		Create your own mind map	
31	Chapter 3	Nothing is impossible but everything is probable	
		Knowing where to start	
53	Chapter 4	Exercise Fx for a healthier you	
		Set your own program	
83	Chapter 5	The Rescue Me Flavour Diet	
		Cook to eat, taste and flavour	
129	Chapter 6	Winemakers, chefs and heavenly flavours	
		Wine food and more wine	
143	Chapter 7	Childhood obesity and the big fat truth	
		Shaping the future	
161	Chapter 8	Baby boomers and a new lease of life	
		Get up and go	
171	Chapter 9	The balancing act of chronic back pain and obesity	
		Lower back pain and rheumatoid arthritis	
181	Chapter 10	The recipe for keeping it off	
		It's your choice	
186	Acknowledgements		
187	References		

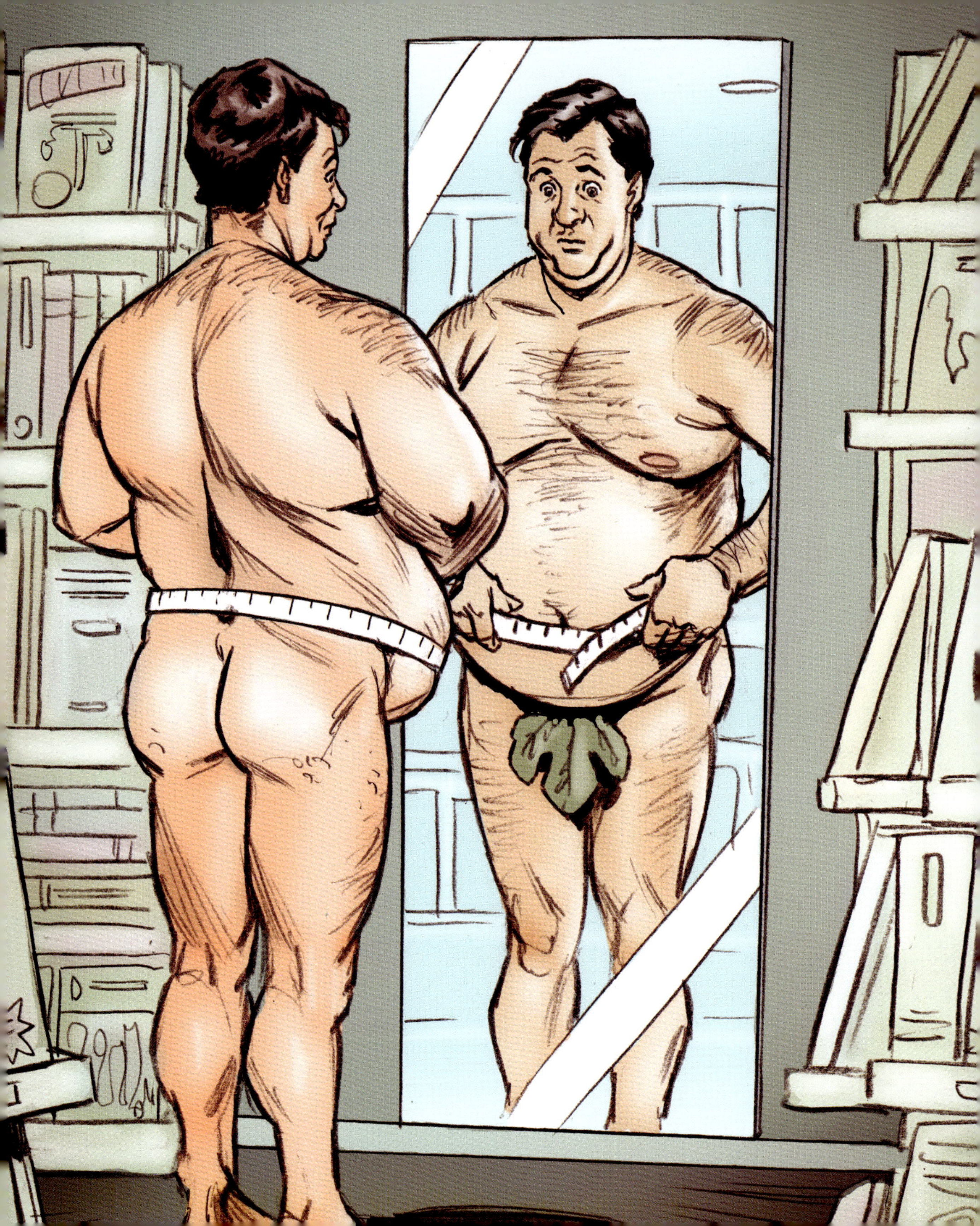

Right now…immediately… take your clothes off and stand in front of the mirror. If you are happy with what you see then get dressed and give this book to someone else.
If the mirror tells you that your body needs a rescue then read on!

RESCUE me   6

Chapter 1

In the raw - obesity at the heart of the problem

Mirror, mirror on the wall

Look at your body shape, your height, weight, physical fitness, heart rate and the way you breathe. These are the basics you'll be considering as you develop the key indicators to assess where your body currently is, determine risk factors and manage your own rescue plan.
Stay with it – it's easy and, more importantly, it's necessary.

The World Health Organisation defines obesity as an accumulation of excess body fat, to an extent that health might be impaired. A precise way to determine your weight category and whether you are obese or not is to use one of the Body Mass Index, or BMI, calculation methods below.

BMI calculation method using imperial measures of height in inches and weight in pounds:

$$BMI = \frac{\text{your weight in pounds}}{(\text{your height in inches} \times \text{your height in inches})} \times 703$$

Example: Bob Living-Stone is 5'10" or 70 inches tall and weighs 251 pounds.
To calculate his BMI he does the following sum:

$$BMI = \frac{251}{(70 \times 70)} \times 703$$

$$BMI = 36$$

The same calculation using metric measure looks like this:

$$BMI = \frac{\text{your weight in kilograms}}{(\text{your height in meters} \times \text{your height in meters})}$$

Example: Betty Living-Stone is 167cm or 1.67 meters and weighs 81kg.
The sum to work out her BMI is:

$$BMI = \frac{81}{(1.67 \times 1.67)}$$

$$BMI = 29$$

After you calculate your BMI you will then know your own weight category.

Weight categories:	BMI
Normal weight	18.5 - 24.9
Overweight	25 - 29.9
Obese	30 - 34.9
Very obese	35 - 39.9
Extremely obese	40 and over

For a quick handy calculator to determine your BMI, log onto www.rescuemeonline.com

The danger signal is the accumulation of belly fat. For men a waist circumference of 40in/102cm is a health risk; for women it is 35in/88cm. As fat accumulates, males tend to develop an apple shape and females a pear. Due to the effects of sex hormones on fat cells, females tend to put more weight under the arms and around the hips and buttocks, whereas with males fat becomes concentrated around the abdomen.

Knowing the enemy is the heart of the problem

The bottom line for obese people is cardiovascular, or heart, disease (CVD). Gaining excess weight can bring with it many complicating health problems, among them high blood pressure, type 2 diabetes, sleeping problems, cancer, abdominal pain, joint pain, and reduced physical function. However, the heart is where the road reaches an abrupt halt. It's the metabolic syndrome and its inflammatory nature that can speed you on your way to this terminal destination.

The metabolic syndrome and a fat abdomen

The metabolic syndrome is a two-word phrase that will become as commonly used as the term heart disease. It is not a single disease process but rather a group of closely related risk factors that lead to a greater chance of CVD. The features of the metabolic syndrome are an excessive amount of abdominal fat, insulin resistance resulting in high blood sugar levels, high blood pressure and poor cholesterol levels. The underlying mechanism is inflammatory, caused by abdominal fat cells (adipose tissue) releasing inflammatory substances called adipokines into the blood stream. These fat cells normally play a healthy role in maintaining blood sugar levels and storing energy for survival needs. But when there is an excessive amount of abdominal fat, these cells can become dysfunctional, leading to the release of the inflammatory adipokines which can cause damage to your body.

The inflammatory nature of the metabolic syndrome can play an active role in the development and maintenance of major diseases such as type 2 diabetes, arteriosclerosis and CVD and is even associated with osteoarthritis. There are also potential implications for menopause (see chapter 8).

RESCUE me | 12

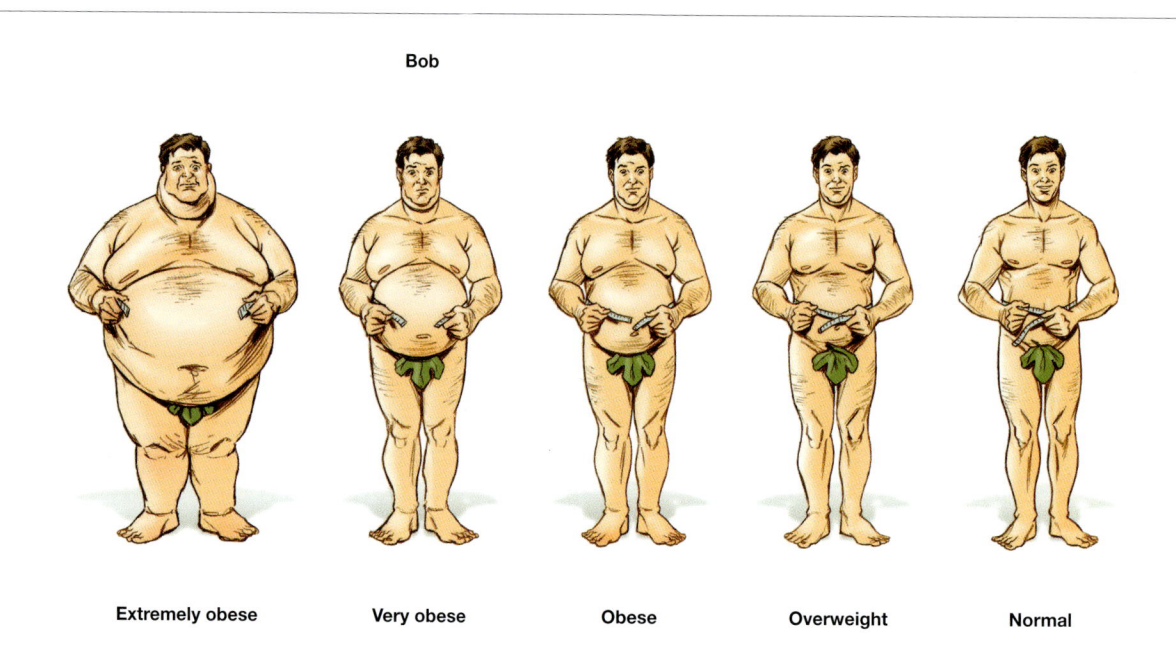

Bob

| Extremely obese | Very obese | Obese | Overweight | Normal |

Bob Living-Stone is currently very obese. He has a BMI of 36 and the amount of abdominal fat he's accumulated (42 in/107 cm) indicates he is well on the way to heart disease, high blood pressure, type 2 diabetes and possible physical impairment of the spine and pelvis. If he keeps heading in this direction he will become extremely obese, with a 1m wide coffin waiting at the end of the tunnel. Putting a rescue plan in place can help Bob rediscover his waistline; to run, move, and discover life with his son and wife again. He can continue his weighty downward spiral or choose a rescue.

Metabolic syndrome occurs when three or more of the following risk factors are present:

1. Abdominal obesity with waist circumference bigger then 40in/102cm (for men) and 35in/88cm (for women)

2. Fasting glucose greater than 110 mg/dL

3. Elevated blood pressure, higher than 130/85 mmHg

4. Decreased high density lipoproteins, or HDLs (these are good cholesterol) – to less than 40 mg/dL for men or 50 mg/dL for women

5. Elevated triglycerides, to greater than 150 mg/dL

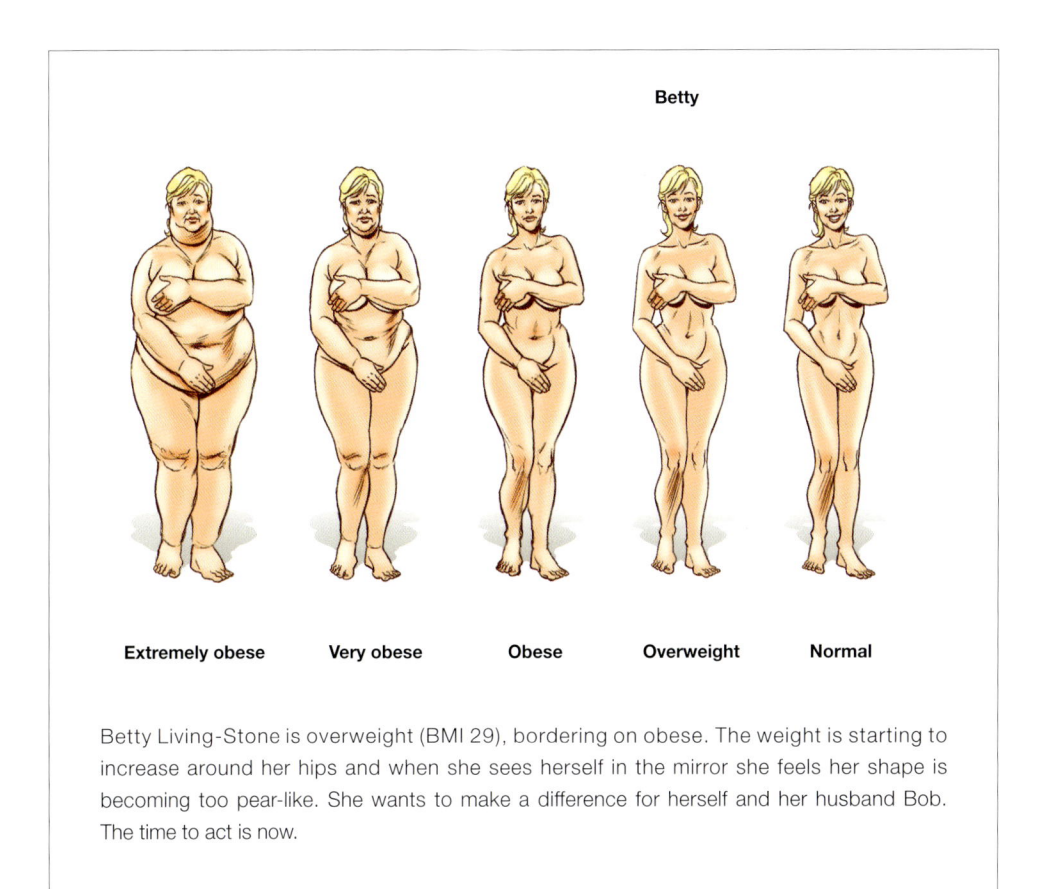

CHAPTER 1 | IN THE RAW - OBESITY AT THE HEART OF THE PROBLEM   13

Betty

Extremely obese   **Very obese**   **Obese**   **Overweight**   **Normal**

Betty Living-Stone is overweight (BMI 29), bordering on obese. The weight is starting to increase around her hips and when she sees herself in the mirror she feels her shape is becoming too pear-like. She wants to make a difference for herself and her husband Bob. The time to act is now.

To get this information you can go to your doctor. However you can easily measure your waist circumference by using a tape measure around the waist line just below the naval or belly button. You can use both BMI and waist circumference to monitor your health as you aim to lose weight.

**When you look in the mirror what do you see?
Which direction will you choose? Right or left?**

Fat, fast food and bad cholesterol on the attack

Abdominal fat and fast food can increase the level of inflammation in your blood to the extent that it affects the health of your heart and arteries. Digesting fast food has been shown to cause an inflammatory response and produce free radicals which are highly reactive molecules which can cause damage to your tissues. Conversely, a healthy meal rich in fruit and fiber does not cause these adverse reactions.

Damage to arteries resulting in heart disease and high blood pressure is due to the imbalance of HDLs which carry cholesterol away from the cells of tissue, and low density lipoproteins, or LDLs, which carry cholesterol into the cells of tissue. Normally the cells use cholesterol for good things like production of hormones, and excessive cholesterol not used by the cell re-enters the blood stream to be picked up and taken away by the HDLs. Arteries become compromised when HDLs are low (as in metabolic syndrome) and LDLs become excessive.

With excessive LDLs in the blood some become damaged by circulating free radicals. The damaged LDLs lodge into arterial walls causing an inflammatory response. Over time the cholesterol they carry builds up on the walls of the arteries and a plaque develops. This leads to the hardening of the arteries also known as arteriosclerosis. Coronary arteries may also become clogged, compromising blood flow and therefore oxygen to the heart muscle, which potentially can cause angina and/or a heart attack.

Insulin to the rescue – but it can only go so far

Insulin is a hormone produced in the pancreas. Its major role is to help regulate blood glucose levels after food intake by transporting glucose into the muscles and fat cells and storing sugar in the liver as a reserve. It also has an important anti-inflammatory role, whereby it can counter the inflammation associated with eating fast food. However, when someone overeats regularly and becomes obese the demand on insulin to balance both continuously high blood sugar levels and inflammatory components that are released from excessive abdominal fat cells can cause the pancreas cells to fatigue. This effects insulin production, contributing to the possibility of type 2 diabetes.

Diabetes

There are two forms of diabetes. Type 1 diabetes is a disease where the immune system attacks the insulin-producing pancreatic cells. As a result less insulin is produced and life-long insulin-replacement therapy is needed.

Type 2 diabetes is the more common form of diabetes. It is an incurable life-long disease marked by high levels of sugar in the blood. It occurs when the body does not respond correctly to insulin. The main problem caused by this form of diabetes

FAT
MUSCLE
IN TROUBLE
TYPE 2 DIABETES
SUGAR IN
INSULIN
LDL
C
HDL
ARTERY
IN TROUBLE
HOME RUN
RESCUE me

relates to the tissues, especially muscle and fat cells, becoming resistant to the effects of insulin. This means sugar cannot enter these cells effectively and the blood sugar level begins to rise. The pancreas over-produces insulin to reduce the blood sugar levels - in vain, however, as the problem is mainly with the cells that insulin acts on. Over time, the pancreas begins to fatigue and to produce less insulin.

In some cases people with type 2 diabetes may need insulin replacement therapy. With a reduction in the amount of insulin being produced and, therefore, in its anti-inflammatory effects, greater inflammation within the body's systems is likely to occur. This once again increases the likelihood of CVD. Other complications of type 2 diabetes include kidney disease, nerve damage, and blindness.

While the damage to the pancreas cells cannot be undone, its impact can be minimised by losing weight, because a smaller fat cell becomes less insulin resistant and produces more of a beneficial hormone called adiponectin. This aids blood glucose regulation by increasing insulin's action.

DIY: With healthy food choices and exercise you can reduce the impact of the metabolic syndrome, type 2 diabetes, arteriosclerosis and CVD.

Improvement in insulin sensitivity can be seen long before weight loss. So get into a self rescue mode even if you exercise and don't lose weight immediately. You will be doing your body a favour.

Genetics and choice

In relation to genetics and obesity, a single gene dysfunction causing obesity is rare. Rather, obesity is a consequence of interactions between multiple genes and the environment. Because of this it is hard to predict obesity through genetics. It is more a game of probability. You can choose what foods you eat and that in turn effects the way your cells respond to the environment you create.

You are what you eat! Does this sound familiar? But there is more to you than food – how do you express and use the energy you obtain from the food you eat? You can use your freedom of choice and give your body a chance to express the right genes through the right choices of food and regular exercise. You've made the choice to read on, so let's continue on to your individual rescue.

Chapter 2
The secret to the rescue

Chapter 2: The secret to the rescue

Losing weight is complicated. At some point you have to 'step up to the plate' and hit the ball home to your family, friends, work colleagues and most importantly to yourself. The time is now. It's a do-or-die game and it starts with one person standing at the plate ready to make a difference. Are you ready to choose a difference, and set your mind on the target? Watch the ball!

Yes, you really can do it. However, first turn your mind to our analogy of the baseball players. They step up to the plate with a history, self-knowledge and confidence that they can hit the ball. They have had hours of practise, training, pre-game talks and analysis; they know the strengths and weaknesses of the pitcher and the aspects of their throwing action that will reveal what kind of ball is likely to be pitched. Standing on the plate they wait, breathe and focus on what needs to be done. They remember the field placement and then concentrate on the pitcher. And then the real fun begins: the pressure and the mind games between pitcher, batter and coaches. The elements for success are there - by the time the bat hits the ball the batter has a sense of where that ball will be going.

The steps to your success are the same as for the baseball player. They involve knowing who you are and why. That means understanding what you are trying to achieve, planning, practising, being aware of your strengths and weaknesses, knowing that success and failures will come, opening your mind to the opportunity to learn and communicate, and developing your ability to be a team player – this is the way for you to win, to lose weight and to become fit.

From a distance weight loss appears simple

Foods contain energy that our bodies burn. The basic unit for the measurement of energy used by the body is called a calorie. Different foods have different calorie counts just as different exercises expend more calories then others. Weight loss occurs when the amount of energy used by the body is greater than the amount consumed. The 'energy in' versus 'energy out' weight control model shows the consequence of eating too much food and not doing enough exercise. It also shows how you can lose weight by eating less and exercising more.

The not so simple truth

Bob is the man standing in the yellow triangle. He is currently very obese. He has a BMI of 36 and puffs hard after walking up four flights of steps. He thinks that losing weight is a simple matter of drinking a little less beer, not eating doughnuts and maybe going for a run several times during the week. But the fact that Bob is still overweight suggests it's not really so simple. Bob does not understand the real issues at hand and has no realistic idea of how to do something about his problem.

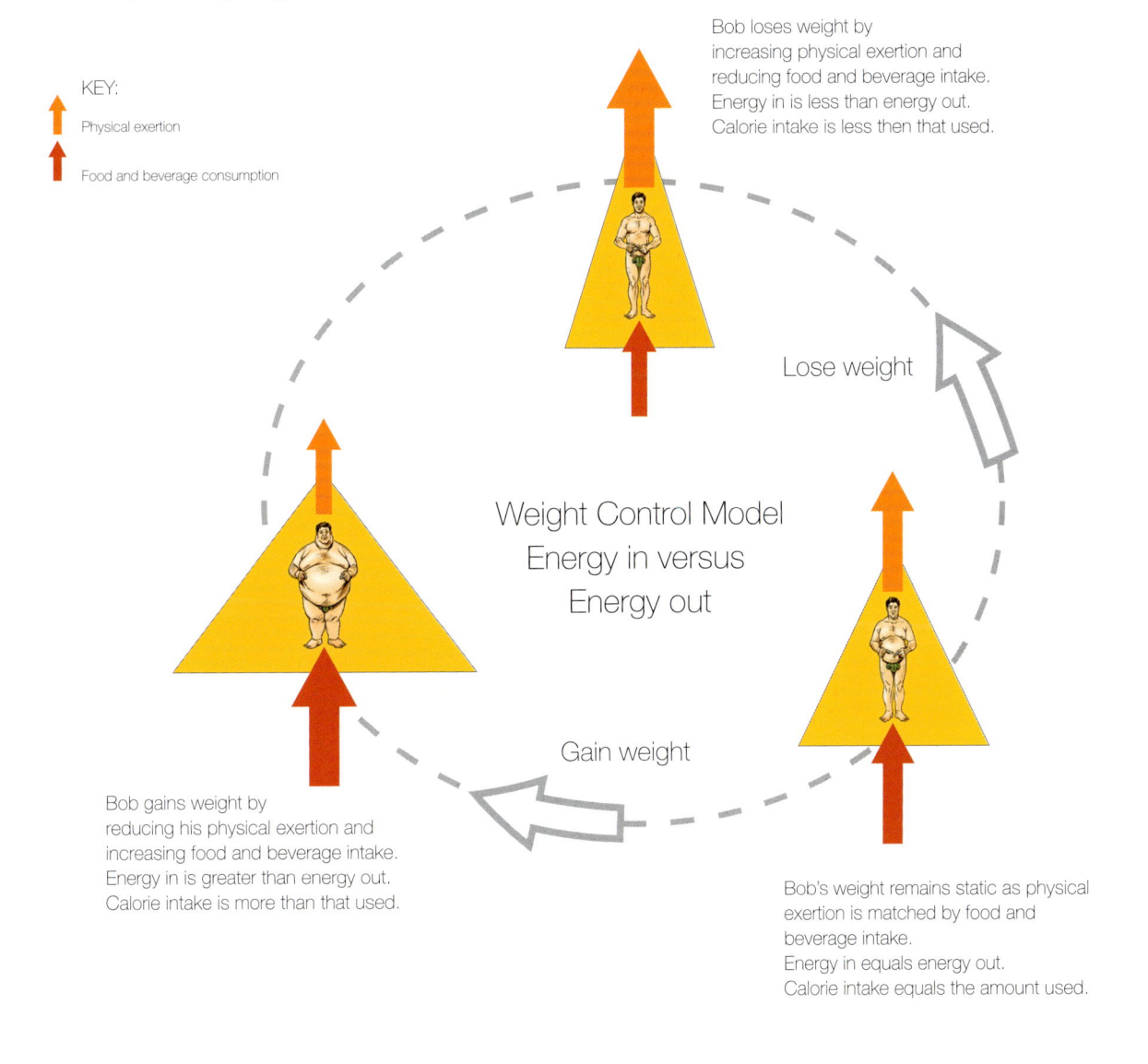

KEY:
Physical exertion
Food and beverage consumption

Weight Control Model
Energy in versus Energy out

Lose weight

Gain weight

Bob loses weight by increasing physical exertion and reducing food and beverage intake. Energy in is less than energy out. Calorie intake is less then that used.

Bob gains weight by reducing his physical exertion and increasing food and beverage intake. Energy in is greater than energy out. Calorie intake is more than that used.

Bob's weight remains static as physical exertion is matched by food and beverage intake. Energy in equals energy out. Calorie intake equals the amount used.

**Understanding yourself is the secret.
Your life is not a dress rehearsal - this is your own reality program and the time to get it right is now. The integration mind map is a diagram that will assist you to discover who you are and why you need weight and exercise planning. Once you know this you will be in control and be able to plan with a firm objective in mind.**

What is the mind map?

Each person who reads this book has their own individual aims for weight loss, wellbeing, health and life circumstances to consider. Your integration mind map offers you a way to make your Rescue Me food and exercise plan suit your needs and helps you get the right people involved. The map works in conjunction with the weight control model of 'energy in' versus 'energy out'. The rules are easy. Have fun with it; don't be precious. Be prepared to laugh and smile at yourself and others!

Creating your own mind map

The integration mind map uses basic shapes and sizes to represent different aspects of your life and their perceived significance. Change the shapes and sizes to suit you. The yellow triangle represents you as an individual.

Step 1. Begin by drawing a yellow triangle, representing you. From base to tip of the triangle represents a gradient of dependency, with the base being dependent and the tip less dependent. For example, food is critical in life so it enters through the base of the yellow triangle.

Step 2. Estimate the size of the arrows for food and beverage consumption and physical exertion. Be honest: are you currently gaining weight, maintaining your weight or losing weight? If you are gaining weight then the 'energy in' arrow (red) will be bigger than the 'energy out' arrow (orange).

Step 3. Draw a genetics triangle, where the three sides of the shape represent the body types of your parents, grandparents and siblings. Overlap this triangle onto the yellow one so it indicates how much you consider genetics contributes to your weight issues. If one or both of your parents are or have been overweight and you feel your body type is similar to theirs, do a large overlap. Consider everything – for example: 'I have my mother's pear-shape hips with a slimmer waist line' or 'I put weight on under my arms or around my back or chest like my father's side of the family.'

CHAPTER 2 | THE SECRET TO THE RESCUE   21

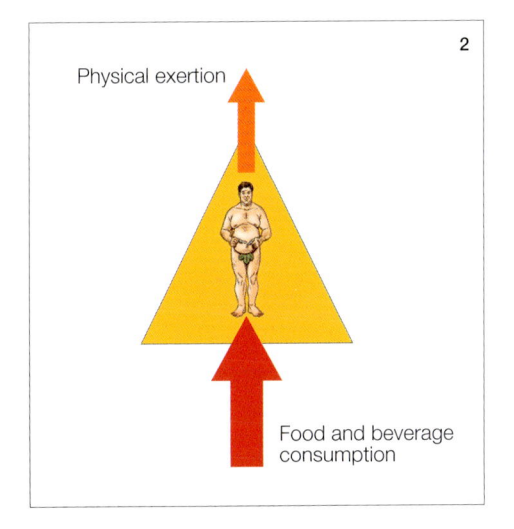

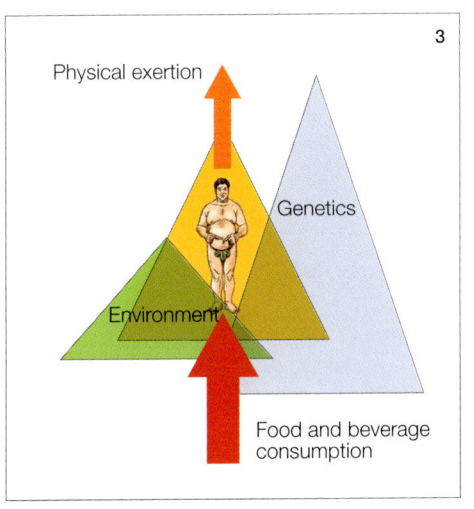

Draw a green environment triangle. This reflects aspects of your life such as socio-economics and the environment in which you live. If you are financially secure, live in a temperate environment conducive to outdoor exercise and you have easy access to good food shopping - and you take advantage of these circumstances, draw a smallish triangle. If you don't fully exploit these advantages draw a larger triangle. The bigger the negative impact, the bigger the triangle.

Next, consider how physical environment interacts with genetic traits. For example: "Both my parents and I have a slow metabolism. My mother and I have had sedentary jobs and are overweight whereas my father did physical work, gaining weight only when he retired." Here a combination of a slow metabolism (genetics) and a sedentary work place (environmental factor) contribute to a faster weight gain.

"Could I change the way my parents' weight gene manifests itself in me if I re-evaluated my work ethic and food choices?" Draw a large overlap if the answer is yes, and a small one if the answer is no.

1. Bob stands in the yellow triangle that represents self

2. Energy in versus energy out

3. Into the mix of me

4. What life demands

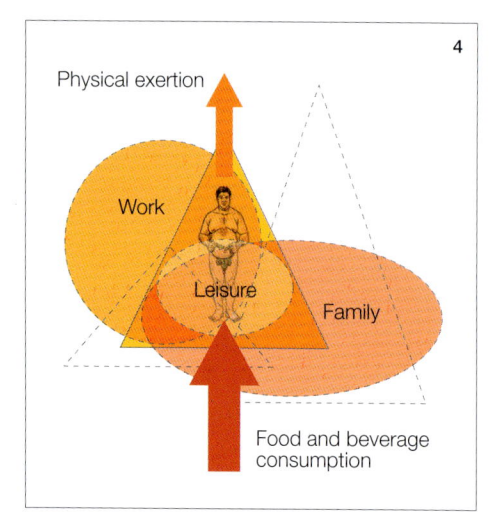

Physical exertion

Work

Leisure

Family

Food and beverage consumption

Step 4. How much time do you give to your family, work or leisure? Draw circles for each. If you work 10 hours a day in an office with very little physical exertion, eating takeaway food because it's convenient, then the work circle will be large and will interact with the red food arrow more than with the exercise arrow. If you work part-time for 12 hours a week and are an at-home mum or dad then the work circle will be small and the family circle larger.

Now determine how much the demands of your work and family affect the way you exercise and eat, then overlap the shapes appropriately. How significant is your occupation? For example night shift workers whose jobs end late may have limited access to healthy food and exercise options. Combined with poor sleeping patterns this may lead to increased fatigue and weight gain.

Finally, draw a leisure circle and layer it appropriately over work, family, environment, genetics, food and exercise. Consider how work affects the time you have for leisure and therefore your choice of leisure activity. For parents, differentiating leisure from family can be hard as leisure time is often spent with the family. Therefore family and leisure circles will overlap significantly.

Step 5. As the pattern of these multiple inter-layered shapes reveals, within yourself you are juggling many competing needs and issues. Life also throws in the unexpected, such as pain, illness and psychological dysfunction. Depending on their severity, these can totally reshape and revalue the factors discussed so far in relation to the concept of you. For instance, if you develop chronic lower back pain you might need to take time off work, which could significantly change your role both at work and at home. Often people with chronic lower back pain cannot exercise effectively and before they know it they are gaining weight.

The expected includes the obligations or rules of conduct associated with religion, culture, values and ethics, social norms, financial responsibility, technology and government policy at local, national and international levels.

The infrastructure of the support services around you, both formal and informal, is also significant as this determines the ease with which you can access health advice, other support and friendship. If you feel your efforts

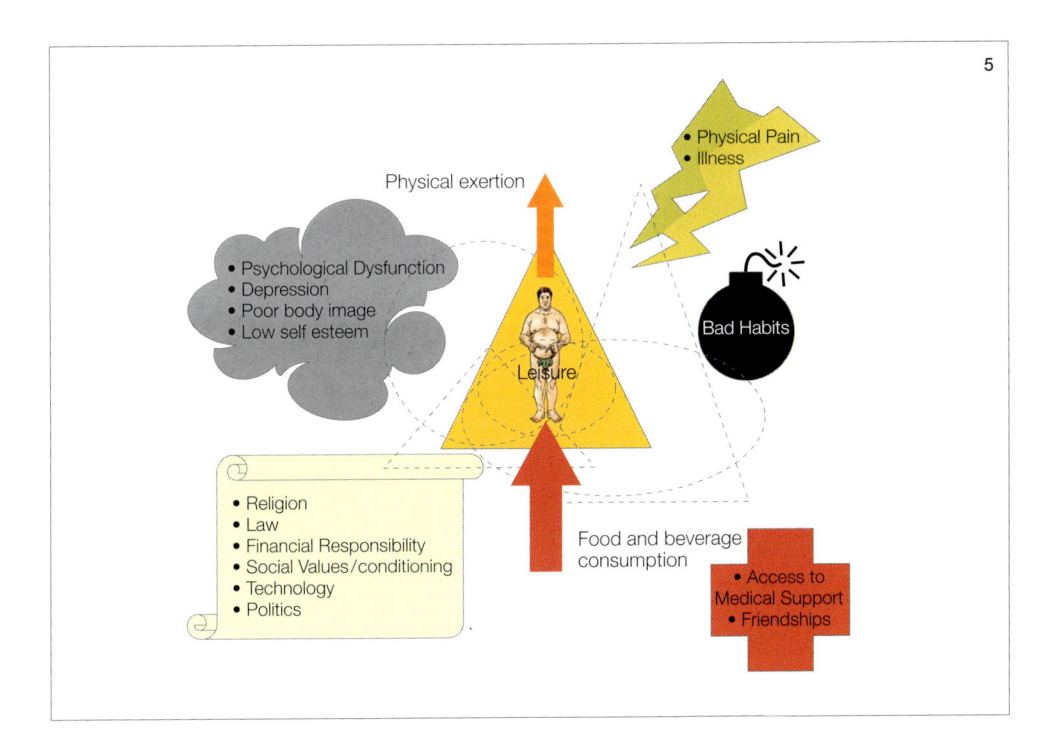

5. The unexpected, expected and infrastructure

to reduce your weight aren't supported by others then to achieve that goal you have to be even more self-motivated. Use your medical doctor in your rescue plan. Not only can they monitor your physical and mental wellbeing but they can help you formulate steps in a rescue plan. They have a network of professionals they can call on to assist you in developing the right mindset.

Bad habits may plague your attempt to lose weight. You may be a chocoholic or have a sweet tooth that at times leads to binge eating. Some people smoke, and when they decide to give up for health reasons they may substitute food for cigarettes.

Your change is for life – not just for after Christmas.

Step 6. Sit back and look at your model. Identify the areas that you think create barriers to losing weight and those that can help you achieve it. Put a cross or a tick on them respectively. Write them down on another piece of paper. You need to be prepared to change them, so work out how much of a change is comfortable for you and your situation. Finally, write a summary of the causes of your obesity problem. As well as discovering some of the reasons for your weight gain, you should be able to identify some solutions to the problem. Now make the choice to change for life.

Now make yourself accountable by telling your family and friends that you have adopted a new plan in order to achieve your target. You have made a commitment to yourself and to them. Tell yourself and them again! You're locked in - you're going to do it so let's start by understanding the complexity of life (it's quite simple really and the secret's out!).

An example to assist you with your plan.

Here is the way Bob evaluated his life to produce his particular mind map:

+ Positive Results

- ☑ Both Bob's parents and grandparents were relatively lean in build, so genetics does not seem to be a factor.

- ☑ Bob lives in a comfortable home in an area with good opportunities for exercise and plenty of food shopping options.

- ☑ Bob's wife Betty is keen to change things at home to help both of them lose weight. Bob and Betty realise that their son Bud is a little too heavy for his age and are worried that he doesn't engage in active play much. The family has a mindset for change.

− Barriers to Losing Weight

- ☒ Bob doesn't shop or cook at home as Betty does all that. He eats fast food for lunch and sometimes goes to work without breakfast, so he has a few pick-me-up snacks during the day.

- ☒ He does little exercise, apart from kicking the ball with Bud on the weekend and mowing the lawn every second week. He knows he needs to do more. He can't remember the last time he ran for more than five minutes.

- ☒ Work is very demanding as he is in a project management role. The company has some big projects that require him to work extra overtime. There is a gym at work, but he doesn't use it.

- ☒ Bob thinks he has no 'medical issues' other than being two or three sizes too big. He is a candidate for metabolic syndrome but no one has had a chance to tell him as his last medical check up was eight years ago.

Bob's summary

Bob feels his weight gain is due to too much stress and long hours at work. These leave him feeling exhausted and frustrated. He drinks beer to calm down at night and likes coming home to watch television so that he doesn't have to think. He isn't motivated to exercise at the end of the day and carries this feeling through into the weekend. He sees no way out. He doesn't seek help and doesn't realise he is a candidate for type 2 diabetes and high blood pressure.

Bob has access to all the resources he needs to change. But, together with Betty,

CHAPTER 2 | THE SECRET TO THE RESCUE   25

he has to make deciding to change a priority. He has to reconsider his working conditions, working hours and so on. Is there an opportunity to exercise at lunchtime or while he's at work – for example, by getting out of his chair and walking around every 30 minutes?

Bob and Betty are now developing a food and exercise program for the family, which answers the questions they uncovered in Bob's integration mind map.

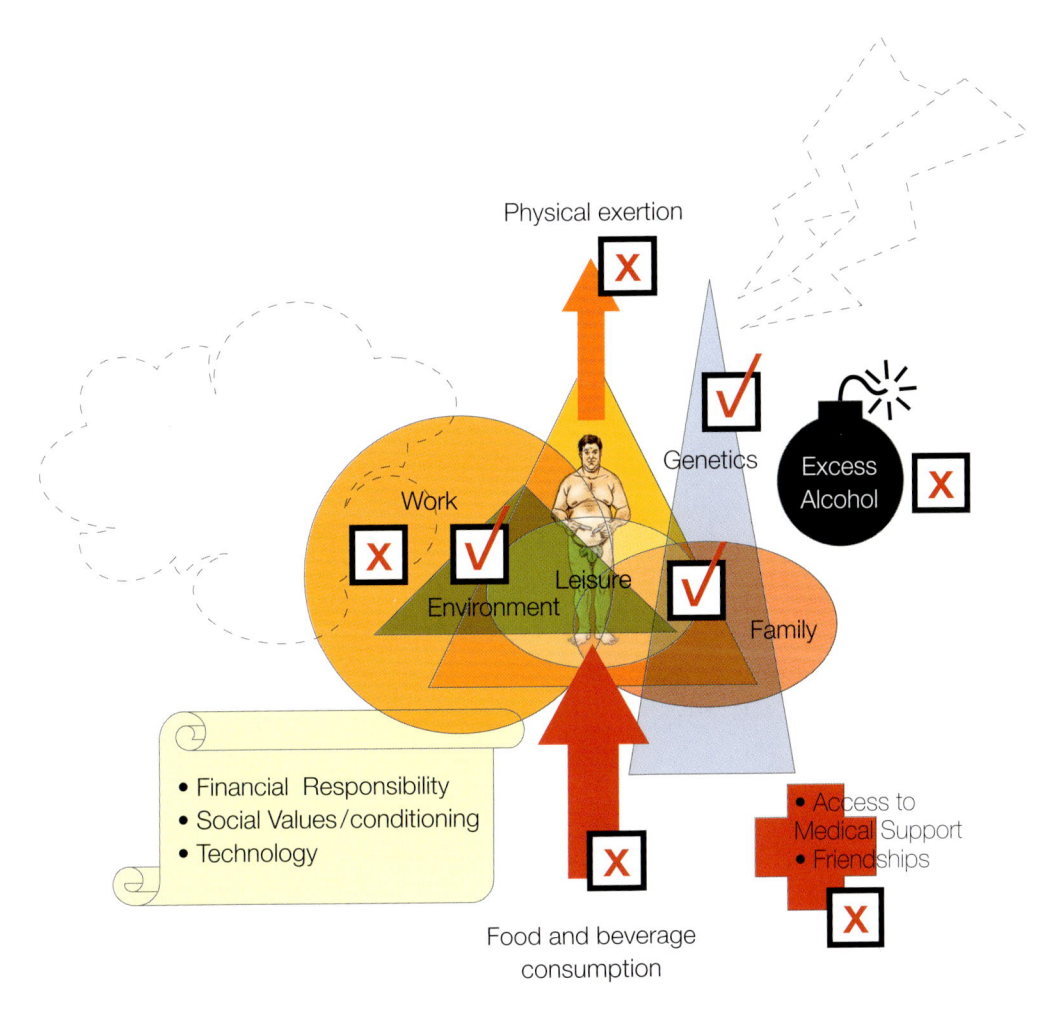

Physical exertion

Work

Genetics

Excess Alcohol

Leisure
Environment

Family

- Financial Responsibility
- Social Values/conditioning
- Technology

- Access to Medical Support
- Friendships

Food and beverage consumption

Bob's mind map results showing ticks on factors that do not contribute to weight gain and crosses on factors he identifies as barriers to weight loss.

Running the gauntlet - the best way through

There are many approaches to diet management for weight loss, among them high carbohydrate/low fat, high protein/low carbohydrate, and the low glycemic index (GI) diet. These diets all focus on controlling energy creation and storage. The bottom line of all diets is really that you need to control your appetite, know when enough is enough and make food choices that give you satiety or a feeling of fullness early in the meal.

The key to diet management is a regular and controlled eating pattern. Three meals a day is a great start. The body needs to develop a regular rhythm of eating so it can make necessary adjustments to food quantities at each meal.

Breaking this regularity and skipping meals can cause the body to go into survival mode, resulting in binge eating. The body is unsure about when the next meal is coming; its response, quite literally, is to save some extra food for a rainy day. When you miss a meal, the effects may not be felt until the next day. This becomes a further danger point, as the body aims to catch up on missed opportunities.

Controlled eating is about planning meals and making a decision to buy whole foods to satisfy appetite. We live in a world where food has been made convenient, comes pre-prepared and if we can't cook it there's always a place to get it and get it fast! Convenient pre-prepared meals and condiments are becoming ever more popular as they 'allow' us to maintain our busy lifestyles.

It may seem easier to just pour a pre-prepared sauce over your food rather then make your own. But the consequence of these decisions is the de-skilling of your own cooking. You lose your ability to effectively control what goes into your meals and to portion your food efficiently. By diminishing your association with and experience of food your sense of taste, your response to flavour and your feelings towards the food will suffer. As the quality of our food experience is reduced, the body responds by increasing the quantity of food needed for satiety.

When you prepare food yourself you learn the 'this goes with that' of cooking through the trial and error of first-hand experience. It may mean a few burnt pans or meals that are less than perfect. But this will be counterbalanced by the serendipitous eureka/nirvana results. You learn the power of mixing ingredients to create a live 'food experience'.

When you prepare food, cooking becomes an experience worth sharing, worth teaching, and worth talking about. We all know the difference between a homemade birthday cake and buying one at the local franchise cake shop. When food is prepared specially for you it is valued more by all who share it. If the cake turns out a flop - well, you have something to talk and laugh about the next day.

In Chicago the average distance from a school to the nearest fast-food restaurant is approximately 520 meters which is a five minute walk. Is it any wonder that the city is experiencing a childhood obesity epidemic and that sales from fast food restaurants increased by 300 per cent between 1977 and 1996?

Energy in – choosing wisely

The reason to choose fresh wholesome food is that it gives it a chance to do the job it was designed for - to satisfy your hunger and keep you healthy. Refined foods have their place; however, they should be used sparingly in a 'less is more' fashion.

Health concerns related to the additives or processing methods used to produce refined foods are another reason to use them in moderation. The hydrogenated oils containing trans fatty acids (trans fats) used by manufacturers to improve the texture of foods are one example of this. It's now well documented that trans fatty acids may increase the risk factor of heart disease, arteriosclerosis, stroke and diabetes because they increase LDLs, decrease HDLs and increase inflammation in the body. Oils used by manufacturers which are high in trans fatty acids include palm oil, palm olein oil, coconut and soy bean oils commonly used in French fries and mass produced cakes and donuts.

While organic food is often more expensive than food that's conventionally produced, the extra cost is likely to mean you value the food more and manage it more efficiently in your preparation and cooking. Organic produce may have a higher nutritional content, perhaps because synthetic fertiliser-grown crops yield produce with a higher water content that dilutes their nutrient levels. Organically grown meat may be leaner – not always, however; the synthetic protein used in pigs' diets, for example, makes conventional pork a little leaner.

You know the 'organic' product is on the move when supermarkets start stocking their own line of organics on the shelf. So be discerning with your purchases and budget for freshness first.

Buying food does require management decisions. You need to juggle concepts of freshness versus pre-prepared, quality versus quantity, whole food versus refined, organic versus conventional, planned versus convenient. If you cook, shop and eat in group situations, others need to be considered in the decision-making process. For your children it may be simply getting them to learn to set the table, peel some vegetables and stir a safe pot. For your partner and friends it will mean sharing experiences and teaching each other.

Many countries provide a recommended food guide for balanced eating. In America there is a pyramid with the "steps to a healthier you" (mypyramid.gov). Canada has the food guide to healthy eating in the form of a rainbow (hc-sc.gc.ca) and Australia publishes a pie chart in the shape of a pizza promoting a variety of foods for everyday consumption (health.gov.au).

Energy out - physical exertion

Exercise is the other critical part of the losing weight equation and has many additional benefits: mood enhancement, cardiovascular fitness, functional ability, co-ordination, reduced health risks plus interesting effects on your sense of taste, food and appetite. Exercise has been shown to decrease hunger, increase perceptions of bitterness and sweetness and result in a higher carbohydrate intake at the expense of fat. People who combine diets with exercise tend to be able to maintain the results and behaviours more effectively in the long-term.

Approximately 70 per cent of adults burn energy at a lower exercise or sedentary level. It doesn't take much exercise for you to start losing weight when you are obese or very obese. Even walking at a pleasurable pace is enough to get a noticeable result.

As the rising incidence of obesity worldwide indicates, people of all ages are exercising less. This is likely to be due not just to lifestyle changes but to lack of knowledge about how to exercise. In fact, not knowing how to exercise may be the most challenging obstacle to a person's success.

It could be that people underrate the degree of difficulty associated with various forms of exercise and therefore failure comes early.

People often do not realise that a sedentary lifestyle not only de-conditions your body but de-trains it also. How many of us mistakenly believe that to start an exercise program it just takes a pair of shoes, a running route, a gym or a bike and you're off - only to find that the exercise program grinds to a dead halt when the knees start hurting, the back goes into pain and the body says: "It hurts so much I will be in a wheelchair by Wednesday."

The de-conditioning that occurs if regular exercise is reduced leads to a loss of muscle mass, strength, flexibility, range in joints and cardiovascular fitness. De-training affects your ability to co-ordinate your body and carry out activities in a reliable and accurate fashion.

For example, if you played ball sports three days a week when you were at school and 10 to 15 years later you decide to take it up again, you will notice how de-conditioned you are, with much less strength, power and endurance than you once had. De-training will be reflected in a reduced ability to pivot and turn, kick, hit or catch accurately, stay on your feet and to run with a smooth stride. The combination of de-conditioning and de-training often leads to injuries and development of poor technique, both of which may make it hard for you to fully enjoy your exercises.

The Rescue Me exercise program in chapter 4 shows you how to exercise and to endure! You will learn about the five Es: exertion, execution, enjoyment, evaluation and endurance. The program will start you at a level that is appropriate to your skills and physical conditioning. It then takes you on a process of re-conditioning and re-training, offering different styles of exercise for diversity and convenience.

To lose weight effectively, your exercise program does not need to be strenuous, but it does need to be regular and interesting; just as interesting as your cooking plan, as they are both part of the secret!

Chapter 3

Nothing is impossible but everything is probable

If you have young children, one parent may have to stay behind while the other exercises. But this will have to be counterbalanced somewhere else. If you are taking the children training, then try and find a way to do your exercises at the same time, either by getting involved or by using the facilities on your own. Write down how you can put at least three to six hours aside to exercise per week. Make the choice and then give it a go. Also consider transport and how long it takes to get to your gym, pool, walking or running route or the exercise studio. If you time your exercise well, you may find the hour spent in a gym after work means you spend half an hour less sitting in peak hour traffic.

What type of exercise is right for you is highly individual or, in a family scenario, group specific. Choices often have to factor in what resources are available. What facilities are close to your home or work? They might include walking routes, bike routes, gyms, pools, golf ranges, dance halls, martial arts halls, boxing gyms, beaches, ski fields, anything! Write them down. Consider all the options and then choose where you would like to start.

Don't feel you have to limit yourself to one option. If you choose to exercise three hours only per week, then just one option is viable as it's important to develop the strength and skill you need for that particular exercise. However, if you can do more than three hours, consider additional forms of exercise, allowing you to cross train and diversify your movement options and skills. We suggest that you start with one or two exercise choices, progressing up to three over time. Look at your list of options and tick the three that interest you most.

Everyone has differing skill levels and experiences of exercise. Someone who has never participated in exercise is starting at a different point to someone who exercised frequently when they were younger, got out of the habit and has become de-conditioned and overweight.

The person who used to exercise will have a body memory of exercises and will progress at a faster rate as a result. They must still step into a program slowly, as it takes time to recondition the muscles, nervous system and the joints. Someone with no history of exercise will find their body requires more time to become skilled and to develop co-ordination. Don't be afraid to start, as the potential for developing skill is very high!

Stage 1: Basic eFx

People who are not confident movers, and are considering exercise for health reasons only.

- Have never exercised.
- Do not do regular exercises.
- Get puffed at the sight or thought of walking up a hill.
- Can only exert themselves in exercises for 30 minutes before fatiguing.
- Are not confident to remember exercises.
- Find it difficult to visualise or describe an exercise.
- Would not consider dancing that requires you to repeat a sequence of three to four dance steps.
- Need cueing or verbal support to learn an exercise.
- Have poor health and fatigue quickly.
- Have significant joint pain or restriction causing a reduction in physical abilities and exertion.
- Have poor balance and feel unsafe riding bikes outdoors and walking on uneven or slippery surfaces.
- Feel de-conditioned, de-trained or unskilled in movement.

eFx questionnaire score 0-20

Stage 2: Intermediate eFx

People who are self motivated and feel that exercise is an important part of their day.

- Exercise at least three times a week.
- Exercise to build your body strength and skill.
- Have an exercise plan.
- Participate in one or two different types of exercises.
- Can repeat exercises if shown once.
- Can describe to a friend how to do basic exercises.
- Feel confident to walk into a gym or new exercise group and partake in the exercise.
- Can repeat three to four dance steps.
- Have good physical health and can exert themselves at a mild to moderate level consistently for 45 minutes to one hour.
- Feel safe riding bikes, or walking on uneven ground.
- Participate in some group sports or activities at a social level.
- Feel as if you have a moderate level of body awareness, co-ordination and rhythm.

eFx questionnaire score 21-35

Stage 3: Progressive eFx

People who love to exercise and explore different types of movements. Organise social events that require exercise.

- Exercise three or more times a week.
- Partake in a range of different exercises to challenge their physical abilities and maximise performance.
- Regularly evaluate their program.
- Can do a series of exercises without being shown requiring a verbal description only.
- Seek out new ways to exercise to diversify their current program.
- Can instruct others in exercises confidently.
- Can remember several dance steps and feel co-ordinated enough to dance with several different partners.
- Have good health and can exercise at a moderate to high exertion for 45minutes to one hour.
- Will partake in group sports or activities at a competitive or physically challenging level.
- Are interested in the philosophy of exercise.
- Have a moderate to high degree of body awareness, co-ordination and rhythm.

eFx questionnaire score 36-50

The exercise life raft determines the exercise skill level that is suitable for you to begin the rescue eFx program.

Consider these stages before filling out the eFx questionnaire and compare your score.

RESCUE me

eFx in action	BASIC eFx	INTERMEDIATE eFx	PROGRESSIVE eFx
POOL	Pool walking	Flippers	Lap swimming
	Noodle exercises	Stroke correction	
	Kickboard exercises	Interval lap swimming	
WALKING and RUNNING	Walking on the flat 15 minutes	Walking on hills and inclines	Bush walking moderate to hard
	Walking for 60 minutes	Fire trails	Running drills
	Interval walking	Bush walking mild difficulty	Run intervals
		Jogging intervals and distance	Run distance
BIKE RIDING	Stationary bike	Spin bike	Off-road bike
		On road bike	
PILATES	Pelvic curl	Single leg stretch	Side bend
	Chest lift and hula	Double leg stretch	Leg pull
	Spinal twist	100s	Teaser
	Roll ups	Full back extension	
	Rolling	Front support	
	Back extension	Pike	
	Lateral strength and stability		
GYROKINESIS®	Chair and floor exercises	Chair and floor exercises	Chair and floor exercises
GYROTONIC®	Pulley-tower exercises	Pulley-tower exercises	Pulley-tower exercises
	Sideways arch		
GYM	Machine bench press	Latisimus dorsi (lat) pull down	Barbell bench press
	Machine seated rows	Triceps extensions	Barbell upright rows
	Pectoral (pec) deck	Standing split pulleys chest press	Barbell military press
	Machine leg extensor	Standing split pulleys flyes	Dumbbell bicep curls
	Machine hamstring curls	Low single pulley upright rows	Dumbbell flyes
	Machine leg press		Rack barbell squats
	Machine calf raises		Rack barbell lunges
BOXING	Mitt and bag work	Learn punching technique	Combinations
	Continuous hitting	Basic combinations	Defense work
		Start foot work	Sparring
		Skipping	
DANCE	Beginners class	Keep going	Never stop
EXERCISE IS EVERYWHERE	Housework/gardening/mowing	Getting fitter - maybe doing it all a bit quicker	Even fitter now, I can see an end to that list Time for some leisure activities

Working with the eFx program

This specifically aims to give you exercise options that you can integrate into your life according to the time you have, exercise facilities available to you and your skill level. We also show you how to integrate a variety of different movement programs into a single hour's work out. By combining different forms of exercise you can set a sustainable pace and maintain interest in movement throughout your life. Do not limit your body or mind to any one movement style or philosophy. Movement is universal and for everyone. There is no one way or time to start.

The eFx program is based on skill and body condition. There are three eFx categories: basic, intermediate and progressive. Use the eFx life raft chart opposite to decide what category you belong to, according to the set of exercise skills that best describes you. This will help you determine the types of exercise you can integrate into a program.

The Rescue Me eFx program includes different types of exercises for you to consider. They are pool, walking, running, bike riding, Pilates, Gyrokineises, Gyrotonic, gym, boxing, dancing, winter sports and everyday activities.

Within these different types of exercise you can work in a way that suits your skill level, as shown in the eFx in action table. Be aware that if you are in the progressive eFx category that you can still do the exercises suggested in the basic and intermediate eFx category. In fact, the more advanced you become at movement the more you realise how important the basic exercises are in encouraging full body movements. You have to be more accurate, precise and rhythmical with these exercises compared to a beginner.

Losing weight with the five Es: enjoyment, exertion, endurance, execution, and evaluation

Your body needs to be challenged and stimulated. Normally it is very lazy and very happy to let you give up and return to your past norm. Using the five Es allows you to continually challenge yourself and maintain interest in exercising.

Enjoyment of exercise is important for success but it may take some time before you experience it. The eFx program presents a variety of exercises to choose from; start with the one you think you would 'like' and then do it. Evaluate how much you enjoyed it, and what you enjoyed. Consider who you exercised with, where you went, the instructions given, the social environment, and your overall feeling about the movement style. All these factors are critical to enjoyment.

eFx in action (opposite page) outlines the range of exercises you can put into your own program based on your skill level.

Bob Living-stone eFx Plan

Where	What	When	How
Office	*Gyrokinesis* Arch and Curl Wave	Monday Wednesday Friday	Three times per day 6 times 6 times
	Walk	Tuesday Thursday	Lunch 20 minutes
Weekdays after work with Betty	*Gym* Warm up – exercise Bike Machine bench press Machine Leg Press *Pilates for Abdominals & Back* Chest lift Roll ups swimming	Monday Wednesday When Bud goes to baseball practice	1 hour Exercise Bike-Interval spin 3 sets 15 reps - 30kg 3 x 15 - 40kg 10 repetitions 6 repetitions 20 seconds 25 beats
Weekend with Betty and Bud	*Bike Riding*	Every second Saturday	30 minutes On flat around park on bike track
Weekend with Bud	*Baseball practice-* work on his catching and hitting	Saturday or Sunday morning when Betty goes to Pool.	30 minutes
Weekend	*Bush walking*	Public Holidays	Easy fire trails

The Rescue Me Flavour Diet

So often you pick up a diet book and come quickly to the chapter on cooking. There in front of you are dense pages of recipes and calorie tables. It looked good in the shop but in the kitchen it's nearly impossible to embark on the program, let alone sustain it for more than a few weeks.

In the book store your eyes were caught by the pictures of food and by the hard-sell on the front cover. You liked some of the ideas and maybe you felt that you could use some of the basic recipes in your current cooking, but it's too hard to do without real motivation. You don't have the ingredients and you don't want to cook 21 meals in a week! Pretty soon the book ends up on the shelf with all the others.

What you need is an overall plan to lose weight and a method to keep it off. You generally like a degree of routine and predictability: you have five or 10 meals that you cook from memory, and a few others in the 'special occasions or weekends' category which take extra effort and preparation.

In fact, recognising the ways in which past diet plans have been unsustainable may be a great place to start. Were they too complicated and too demanding to fit into your life?

The Rescue Me Flavour Diet is designed to be sustainable. It develops your skills slowly and in a way that will change you forever. Isn't that what you are searching for?

Instead of leaving you alone with a recipe book our Flavour Diet gently teaches you to shop in a more intelligent way and to be a better cook, in fact to become the good cook you thought you'd never be. The plan considers the big picture: family, work, leisure, food and exercise, bad habits and your budget. You will recognise that to change yourself takes effort from everyone. Too many cooks won't spoil the broth they will make it that much richer! Share the load and you will all feel the rewards.

The Flavour Diet aims to reinvigorate your desire to properly manage your diet through a process of substituting flavour and quality for quantity. Flavour is not a sense and should be clearly distinguished from taste. To enjoy a flavour to its fullest, all the senses need to interact with each other. Max Lake, an internationally recognised Australian food and wine expert and author in the area of taste and flavour has developed six Lake's Laws of Flavour for the Rescue Me Flavour Diet.

1. Less is more. A paradox of pleasure. Flavour and fragrance are best enjoyed at threshold [just able to be perceived]. This law enhances the beauty of simplicity. There are rare exceptions. More can rarely be more.

2. What we eat tastes of what it eats [or subsists on].

Flavour and fragrance of living things derive from their food source.

3. Mood subdues [flavour and fragrance].

Memory, emotion, and ambience influence appreciation. The attention span must be switched on. If not the flavour is not perceived.

4. Sight dominates smell [except an override like the cautionary smell of burning]. The eye has the first bite.

5. Mixtures. The average person can identify three separate aromas in a mix. A trained sniffer rarely exceeds five. A perfume nose may get even more.

6. Taste is the frame of a flavour, smell is its cladding.

It takes time to discover the truth of flavour and how to implement the laws to the fullest.

The Flavour Diet has three different stages and you can start at any one of these. They are:

Cooking to eat (weeks 1-6),
Cooking for taste (weeks 7-9), and
Cooking for flavour (weeks 10-12).

Over the 12 weeks, the Rescue Me Flavour Diet will take you on a journey that improves your ability to plan, prepare, cook, portion and flavour your food.

The flavour life raft outlines the characteristics and skills which we aim to develop or change. When you finish the program you will have the skills you need to mix and match your own ideas.

Begin by considering your current level of cooking skills. If working in a group, then calculate this for all the members of the family, including the children. To do this, use the criteria outlined in the flavour life raft and the cooking questionnaire.

Working with the Flavour Diet

The Rescue Me Flavour Diet that you will find in chapter 5 is a stepped program designed to slowly develop your cooking skills and diet management.

In **Stage one - Cooking to eat** you cook using ingredients with which you are familiar, such as bottled sauces and dressings. In the first week, you aim to prepare only three stated meals. The rest of the week, continue on as usual. These meals are repeated, and some new meals are gradually included. We introduce you to the first step in our portion control plan, regulating eating to set intervals of the day (breakfast/lunch/dinner) to minimise overeating. The second step is to introduce you to healthy food-matching ideas and to improve your shopping options.

By the end of six weeks, you can prepare or cook breakfasts, lunches and dinners regularly. You will use leftovers to make great lunches, maximising convenience. Your pantry is developed slowly to reflect the

CHAPTER 3 | NOTHING IS IMPOSSIBLE BUT EVERYTHING IS PROBABLE

Stage 1: Cooking to eat	Stage 2: Cooking with taste	Stage 3: Cooking with flavour
Weeks 1-6 of the Flavour Diet	Weeks 7-9 of the Flavour Diet	Weeks 10-12 of the Flavour Diet
People who view food as necessary to satisfy basic needs and instincts. Likes their food but doesn't know how to prepare and cook themselves.	*People who produce tasty meals however still rely on take-a-way as an important element in food planning.*	*People who explore food combinations and who are willing to train their palate further. Friends will love an invitation to your house for dinner!*
No food plan.	Basic food planning skills.	Good food planning skills.
Cooks about two meals per week.	Cooks up to four meals per week.	Cooks at least six meals per week.
Shops once per week.	Shops at least twice per week for fresh food.	Shops at least three times per week for fresh ingredients.
Minimal fresh food in the kitchen.	Has a moderate amount of fresh food in the kitchen.	Explores new concepts of flavour.
Gives little consideration to spices and flavours in the cooking.	Uses a basic level of spices and herbs.	Applies Lake's Laws of Flavour.
Regularly uses pre-prepared foods.	Occasionally uses pre-prepared food such as bottle sauces.	Able to make their own pastry, pasta, sauces, dressings and stocks.
Buys take-a-way fast food on a regular basis.	Can use a greater array of cooking styles such as Asian, Italian and Greek.	Able to use a variety of additional cooking styles such as French, Middle Eastern, Asian etc.
No plan to improve cooking skills.	Has a reasonably well equipped kitchen and well stocked pantry.	Uses fresh and seasonal foods.
Basic cooking ability, limited to meals such as "meat and three vege", BBQ and pasta.	Is aware of portion control methods.	Well stocked and prepared kitchen, pantry and fridge.
Poorly equipped kitchen and pantry.	Can use left overs well.	Merge left overs into new meals.
No consideration of portion control.	Happy to sit down at at a table for a meal with family or friends.	Able to portion food to maximise flavour.
Happy to eat on-the-run or in front of the television.		
May binge eat.		
Expected score on the Rescue the Cook questionnaire - between 0 and 20	Expected score on the Rescue the Cook questionnaire - between 21 and 35	Expected score on the Rescue the Cook questionnaire - between 36-50

Flavour life raft determines the cooking skill level that is suitable for you to begin the Rescue Me Flavour Diet.

RESCUE me

The cooking questionnaire is a quick way to evaluate your cooking ability. Complete it weekly or fortnightly during the Rescue Me Flavour Diet.

RESCUE THE COOK QUESTIONNAIRE	SCALE	SCORE
1. Do you cook at least five meals in a week?	0 Never / 1 Rarely / 2 Sometimes / 3 Often / 4 Mostly / 5 Always	
2. Do you shop for fresh cooking ingredients at least three times per week?	0 Never / 1 Rarely / 2 Sometimes / 3 Often / 4 Mostly / 5 Always	
3. Do you prepare meals in advance, such as lunch made at breakfast time, at least twice per week?	0 Never / 1 Rarely / 2 Sometimes / 3 Often / 4 Mostly / 5 Always	
4. Do you save left-overs and re-use?	0 Never / 1 Rarely / 2 Sometimes / 3 Often / 4 Mostly / 5 Always	
5. Does anyone comment on your cooking as being tasty?	0 Never / 1 Rarely / 2 Sometimes / 3 Often / 4 Mostly / 5 Always	
6. Do you eat three meals only per day and no snacks?	0 Never / 1 Rarely / 2 Sometimes / 3 Often / 4 Mostly / 5 Always	
7. Do you apply portion control to your meals?	0 Never / 1 Rarely / 2 Sometimes / 3 Often / 4 Mostly / 5 Always	
8. Are your pantry and fridge stocked with fresh food?	0 Never / 1 Rarely / 2 Sometimes / 3 Often / 4 Mostly / 5 Always	
9. Do you consider your diet well balanced and healthy?	0 Never / 1 Rarely / 2 Sometimes / 3 Often / 4 Mostly / 5 Always	
10. Do you plan your meals to help you lose weight?	0 Never / 1 Rarely / 2 Sometimes / 3 Often / 4 Mostly / 5 Always	
Total Score		/50

meals cooked and minimise the impact on your budget.

Stage two - Cooking for taste further develops the concepts of regular eating, better shopping and more effective cooking. You will be able to make your own sauces and dressings and use a greater variety of ingredients and cooking techniques.

With convenience a constant focus, we introduce the concept of merged meals. This is where part of one main meal is used as a key component of a following meal. For example, the braised vegetables remaining from dinner can become a tasty frittata the following night. Spices, herbs, fresh citrus and wines are combined with food to develop a greater awareness of taste as an important factor when preparing your own meals. Tastier meals are a reward for the effort of cooking. They will help you stay motivated and feel confident about the different foods and styles of cooking you're getting to know.

The portion control plan moves to more specifically changing the amount you eat. We suggest ways to decrease serving size - for example, cut a pizza into twelve pieces rather then eight, and still eat only two slices. Replacing large serving plates with smaller bowls means a visual message of a full plate is conveyed even though the portion is smaller. Chewing food more thoroughly and slowly promotes better digestion and improves satiety.

Stage three - cooking for flavour introduces more complex concepts, such as slow cooking and double baking, food and wine matching and a more diverse use of fresh herbs and spices. The Flavour Diet explores the integration of stocks into different meals, mixing and creating foods sometimes with your hands and an exciting expansion of your knowledge of flavours.

More multicultural foods are introduced, along with imaginative ingredients such as truffle oil, agar agar, duck and rabbit. We explain cooking methods such as double baking, which helps minimise the fat content of meats such as duck, allowing them to be placed on the weight-conscious menu.

The concepts of food merging are further explored, with menu plans featuring merges over several days and into new main meals. Portion control continues to be developed, using the first and fourth of Lake's (six) Laws of Flavour (explained in chapter 7): "the eye has the first bite" and "less is more". We recommend you use bigger plates that demonstrate your ability to present and portion food. This will help develop your skills in food styling, adding value to the concept of quality over quantity. Using this portion control skill signals to your family, friends and to yourself that you are managing and enjoying portion control where less is truly becoming more.

Progressing at the right pace

The Rescue Me Flavour Diet is designed to help an infrequent cook gain the skills and confidence they need to prepare and cook food more often. This includes developing the habit of eating breakfast, lunch, and dinner. The purpose of the three meals a day program is to prevent binge eating or convenience eating when meals (such as breakfast) are missed.

The Flavour Diet repeats meals, to allow you to become familiar with the cooking style and give you an opportunity to practise. Some of the repeat meals are then changed in portioning, or ingredients are removed or new ones added to help you achieve the aim of weight loss. These additions will be found in food tips. Once you are familiar with repeating meals, new dishes or ideas are provided.

In the first stage 'cooking to eat', new dishes are introduced very gradually so you have time to develop your food preparation and cooking habits. On days where meals are not allocated on the plan, you are free to cook, eat or buy meals as you feel is appropriate. You may want to use these unallocated days or meals to practise cooking, presentation and portioning ideas in your own recipes. Or try to follow one of our recipes or food suggestions from memory. Practise is the key to success. As you advance to 'cooking for taste' and 'cooking for flavour', new meals and food ideas are introduced more often.

It's all about easy cooking

The Flavour Diet is presented in different food styles for breakfast, lunch and dinner.

For breakfast the food styles are cereal, breads, fruit, eggs, grains and beverages; for lunch, breads and salads. For dinner: soups, pasta, salads, stir fry, rice, Arborio rice, seafood, grills, traditional meats, barbecue, grains, roasts, pizzas and braised dishes.

These food styles remain the same over the 12 weeks. This is to help you remember what you are cooking and to provide continuity as you progress to cooking advanced dishes and meals. The progressions are simple so that each level of cooking sets a platform for an easy step up to the next level. The food progressions may involve using different meats, spices and base ingredients, varying the preparation and cooking methods, or changing the ethnicity of the food.

Pasta is a good example of this. The first meal in week 1 is pasta with tomato-based Napolitano sauce. Prepare this meal using a bottle of pre-prepared Napolitano sauce, with grated cheese and pepper to taste. In week 9 the style progresses to an oil-based pasta using linguine, prawn, white wine, asparagus, garlic, lemon zest and fresh chili, with fresh dill to top it off. And in week 12 you will learn to make your own pasta and pesto sauce. In summary, over the 12 weeks of the Flavour Diet you move from being a cook who uses dried pasta and a bottle of pre-made sauce to one who makes your own pasta and sauce from scratch.

The convenient cook

Cooking with good time and food management skills makes it easier to maintain a three meal per day Flavour Diet and to implement our food suggestions for losing weight. Gaining these skills is easy with the meal merging featured in chapter 5, whether it involves using leftovers or cooking extra for another time.

An example of a simple merge from one dinner to another is in week 7, where Tuesday night's mustard and rosemary flavoured lamb roast becomes lamb cold cuts and mint salad for lunch the following day. In a more complex merge, veal Zurich, a braised meat dish, is merged into a shepherd's pie.

These meals appear on the food menu in their own category, for example 'merge a dinner into lunch' and 'merge a dinner into another dinner'.

The right place at the right time

To advance through the different stages of the 12 week program, your cooking skills need to be matched by the ability to buy fresh ingredients and by the resources in your kitchen, such as cookware, plates and pantry ingredients.

With this in mind, the Rescue Me Flavour Diet is organised so that cooking skills, shopping skills and kitchen resources improve at the same rate. To be a 'cooking for flavour' cook you need a pantry to flavour from!

To help you, we have provided shopping lists of the fresh ingredients required for each week. To start with, you may only need to shop once a week. As the quantity of fresh food used increases you may need to consider shopping two or three times per week, especially if you're buying fresh products such as seafood.

The pantry is developed more slowly. We've organised what you'll need into three main lists, one for the start of each stage of the Flavour Diet. The expectation is that you'll replace the items on these lists as you start to run out. The pantry for the 'cooking to eat' stage of the plan is basic. If you want, start your shopping for items on the other lists early, so you build your pantry bit by bit. The pantry lists can be found in chapter 5.

RESCUE me

MEAL	FOOD STYLE	COOKING TO EAT Weeks 0-5	COOKING FOR TASTE Weeks 6-9	COOKING FOR FLAVOUR Weeks 10-12
BREAKFAST	CEREAL	Cereal & Fruit	Muesli & Fruit	Oats & Poached Fruit
	BREADS	Toast & Condiments	Toast with Tomatoes & Ham	French Toast
	FRUIT	Fruit Salad & Yoghurt	Poached Peaches/Pears In OJ	Stewed Fruits in Fresh Juices
	EGGS		Scrambled or Poached	Omelet
				Baked Egg Royal
	GRAINS		Pancake with Fresh Fruit	Corn Fritters with Wilted Spinach
	BEVERAGES	Bottled Juice	Freshly Squeezed Juices	Fruit Smoothies
		Coffee	Flat White Skim/Soy	Espresso or Long Black
		Tea Regular Bags	Homemade Fresh Lemon Tea	Green & Black Teas
LUNCH	BREADS	Sandwiches	Pumpernickel	Wraps
	SALADS	Garden Salad	Greek Salad	Waldorf Salad
			Chicken Salad	Pork Fillet & Salad Wrap
			Smoked Salmon, Rocket & Pear Wrap	Duck Risotto
			Chick Pea, Couscous & Falafel Wrap	Chicken Fillet Salad
			Honey Lamb Cutlet Salad	

A menu in action that is based at your cooking skill level for breakfast and lunch.

Choosing a point to start

To best use the menu you have to choose the right starting point for you and the others doing the plan with you. How you pace yourself through the program can then be considered according to the point at which you began. We suggest you assess yourself on the flavour life raft, to find a comfortable starting point.

Remember too that you can make your own timetable for progressing through the plan, repeating weeks where you felt you had difficulty. We suggest that you aim for a 75 per cent success rate before you move onto the next week. If you feel you didn't achieve this then repeat that week. The plan from beginning to end is 12 weeks. If you want to stretch it out, to say 16 weeks, then do so. But make sure you stay on the plan. If you want to be creative try writing your own plan using some of our food suggestions and some of your own favourites.

You may also want to decide on a point at which you're happy with your cooking skills. If you choose not to advance to the 'cooking to flavour' skill level, then repeat the 'cooking to taste' weeks and start incorporating the ideas developed so far into your own cooking repertoire. Learn to write your own plan, try creating merges in advance and write down the fresh ingredients required before you shop. Do this for several weeks so that you can add some of the Rescue Me meals to your own list of remembered favourites.

The beauty of the Rescue Me Flavour Diet is that it can be for one person or for a team of cooks, be it partner, children or friends. This will allow you to divide and conquer by sharing the tasks of shopping and cooking. With a team approach it's important that everyone takes responsibility for good food

A menu in action that is based at your cooking skill level for dinner and dessert.

MEAL	FOOD STYLE	COOKING TO EAT Weeks 0-5	COOKING FOR TASTE Weeks 6-9	COOKING FOR FLAVOUR Weeks 10-12
DINNER	PASTA	Pasta Napolitana	Linguine & Prawns	Pesto Pasta & Pinenuts
		Spaghetti Bolognaise	Rice Paper Rolls & Vermicelli	Chilli Blue Swimmer Crab & Noodles
	SALAD	Garden Salad	Greek Salad	Rocket & Pear Salad
	DRESSINGS	Vinaigrette	Egg Vinaigrette	Lime Juice, Olive Oil & Balsamic Vinegar
	STIR FRY	Hokkien Noodles	Chicken & Snow Peas	Noodles, Mushrooms & Green Beans
	RICE	Curry Chicken & Rice	Honey Lamb Cutlets & Rice	Nasi Goring Indonesian Fried Rice
			Fried Rice	Rabbit Casserole & Boiled Rice
	ARBORIO RICE		Mushroom Risotto	Pumpkin or Beetroot Risotto
	SEAFOOD		Grilled Fish & Salad	Baked Fish & Boiled Rice
	GRILLS	Lamb Chops		BBQ Shrimp & Fish Fillets
	TRADITIONAL MEATS	Steak & Boiled Potatoes	Rack of Lamb	Pork Fillets, Apple Sauce, Asparagus
	BARBECUE	Chevapis & Lamb Chops	Marinated Chicken Thighs	Whole Fish
	GRAINS	Fried Rice	Chick Pea & Coriander Couscous	Baked Fish & Boiled Rice
	ROASTS	Turkey Breast	Leg of Lamb	Rack of Lamb & Mint Sauce
			Roast Lemon Chicken	Double Cooked Duck
	SOUPS	Chicken Vegetable Broth	Minestrone Soup	Moroccan Red Lentil Soup
		Potato & Leek Soup	Mushroom Soup	Cauliflower & White Truffle Oil Soup
	PIZZA	Basic Pizza	Gourmet Pizza	Homemade Polenta Pizza
	BRAISED DISHES		Braised Vegetables	Braised Veal Zurich
				Veal Shepherd's Pie
				Lamb Cold Cuts & Mint Salad
DESSERTS	FRUIT	Fresh Fruit Salad	Summer Berry Pudding	Stewed Fruit in Agar Agar
	FRUIT		Baked Apple with Marsala	Prunes or Pears Poached in Red Wine

choices, even though the program will be paced at a different rate for different people. If you share the cooking and your partner is less experienced than you, then work together to build each other's skills. One approach you might try in this situation is that you both start at the appropriate stage of the plan but in some weeks you allocate three days to the higher level meals cooked by you. This allows your partner to see that he or she can work up into better meal management.

Remember in a team you are only as strong as the weakest link. Encouragement and practise makes the weakest link stronger. If you adopt the motto "nothing is impossible but everything is probable", you can convert your choice for change into a fitter, slimmer healthier you for the long term!

Chapter 4
ExerciseFx for a healthier you

Chapter 4: ExerciseFx for a healthier you

If you have a medical condition see your doctor for a clearance to exercise. Seek trained advice to individualise a program for you.

1. How fast you walk, how deep the water is and the direction in which you walk against the water and its currents determines the resistance of the exercise.

ExerciseFx (eFx) is for everybody. No problem related to age, weight or general physical condition is a total barrier to some form of exercise. If you are aiming to lose weight then exercise, in association with a controlled diet plan, is essential. Toning your body and improving its ability in a range of movements can be highly rewarding.

This chapter explores a range of exercises organised into three eFx stages: basic, intermediate and progressive. Find the exercise style that you enjoy and then start at the appropriate eFx stage.

Write down a program for two weeks to get started. Commit to it, then use the eFx questionnaire to evaluate your progress. Build your program up slowly; think of developing it over six to 12 months. Keep the five Es (enjoyment, exertion, endurance, execution and evaluation) in mind as you progress your program. Set sustainable goals that fit into your lifestyle.

AQUACISE

Exercising in the pool is a great place to start. The water can be used to support the body, as a resistance to push or pull against, and as a medium to create currents that challenge balance and torso strength. A pool with water depth between waist and chest line allows you to walk, lunge, run, do kickboard and noodle resistance, endurance and torso stability work - and to swim. The pool provides a particularly supportive medium for people who have difficulty walking on land due to discomfort, pain, poor functioning ability, low endurance and low skill.

Basic aquacise eFx

1. Walking in water can be done forwards, backwards or sideways.

To increase the speed of walking and your exertion level, use your arms to pull yourself through the water. To build up torso and leg strength, try walking with your hands above your head.

2. Try walking forward at a pace that produces a current behind you, then feel the resistance it creates when you change direction to backwards walking. The effect of currents can be increased, particularly when working in a group. Walk in a circle to create whirlpools or figure eights and zigzags for cross currents.

3. The noodle can be used for spinal rotations, single leg stability and deep water cycling. Spinal rotation helps build the strength and flexibility of the spine. Single leg stability can be practised in the centre of the pool or with your back against the wall. Push down on the noodle with your foot to do a leg press. To increase the challenge, try two noodles under one foot.

Cycling involves wrapping the noodles under the arms. Better to have two so they can go front and back. Cycle the legs in front of the body or under the body to increase the challenge. You may also lean back in this position to do some kick work.

2. Creating currents challenges you by pulling you along with it and then creates considerable resistance when you change direction to move against it.

3. Noodles are excellent aids for resistance, stability and cardiovascular work.

4. Kickboards can be used for more than just lap swimming!

4. The kickboard can be used to increase the water's resistance and your exertion levels when you are walking. Simply hold it in front of the body, pushing it into the water with straight arms as you walk forwards and pulling it against the water as you go backwards. To give the abdominals and arms a workout, squat down in the water, pushing and pulling the board in front of you. Try and do 30 to 40 push pulls in a minute then change to 30-40 push downs for the next minute.

For stability work, and for the daring, try balancing one foot on the board and doing a leg press. Be careful of the 'flying board' – don't let it slip from under your foot and out of control.

5. Use the kickboard for swimming practise as well: hold it in front of the body to do freestyle and breaststroke kicks and on the chest for backstroke kicks.

Intermediate aquacise eFx

Swimming can be quite a complicated activity to learn. With freestyle, ask a swimming coach to show you how to use flippers so you can develop a kicking rhythm which maintains the buoyancy and the streamline of your body. You may use a kickboard for single arm strokes to help develop your glide, reach and ability to pivot through the water. Then you can put these together into a rhythmical stroke with breath control. Start with interval training where you swim half a lap and then walk back to the start. Build to a full lap of freestyle and then return doing breaststroke. Rest for 30 seconds and then repeat.

Progressive aquacise eFx

Once you can swim small distances you should be able to build up the endurance to do freestyle lap swimming. It doesn't happen

5. Swimming into action with a board, flippers and a good style.

6. Father and daughter enjoying a few laps.

overnight but with enough practise you may one day find yourself diving off the blocks with new enthusiasm.

WALKING

Don't underestimate the strength your body can develop by walking between 30 to 60 minutes a day. For those who are extremely or very obese, walking for pleasure at a light to moderate exertion level is enough to start losing weight. For people in the obese to overweight category, walking is only effective for weight loss if the exertion level is increased. This means being prepared to 'puff' or be slightly short of breath and working up a mild sweat.

Basic walking eFx

Begin by walking on the flat for 15 to 20 minutes two to three times per week for two weeks. Then gradually increase the time to 30 minutes. If walking is the only exercise you do then aim to get up to 60 minutes walking per day, five times a week. If you cannot put the time aside in a single block, then several smaller walks is fine (for example, twice a day for 30 minutes).

Once you have increased the duration of your walks, introduce interval walking. Walk at a fast pace (moderate exertion) medium pace (moderate to light exertion) and a slow pace (light exertion).

You could try 50 steps at a medium pace, then 25 steps fast, 50 steps medium and 25 slow. Repeat the cycle. Changing pace requires the body to accelerate or decelerate, which expends more energy.

Regular walking can be a good way to keep your exercise program moving.

Intermediate walking eFx

Incorporate stairs and hills with mild to moderate gradients into your route. Exercise at a moderate intensity, keeping it steady to allow your body to adapt to the new challenges. Interval walking is an effective way to increase your exertion level, particularly when walking fast up hills. Become more stair conscious. Whenever you're somewhere with a choice of stairs versus escalator, use the stairs.

Progressive walking eFx

Challenge yourself by walking on uneven surfaces such as fire trails, bush trails, or in large parkland spaces. This breaks the regularity of stride length, leg lift height,

Walk on both sides of the road as the pavement's slope can make you walk with your body on an angle which can irritate back or leg problems.

When bushwalking wear safe shoes and appropriate clothes. Take a backpack to carry plenty of water and safety items.

exertion, leg drive and pace and makes different demands on your balance. Many cities have trail walks; it just takes a little investigation and time to get to the right place. Joining a walking club will help increase your motivation and introduce you to different walking ideas and options.

RUNNING

Running can vary in speed from a light trot, to jogging, running and then sprinting. The faster the movements become, the more accurate you have to be with your technique and form.

Intermediate running eFx

Jogging involves running at a moderate exertion level and speed and is often done over medium to long distances. Your first jog should be for a short distance on the flat, with interval jogging. Start on a sports ground, running one lap and walking the second lap for recovery. Aim to run six laps to begin with (three in one direction and three in the opposite direction). You will find you that you can build up to 10 laps quite quickly over the next two weeks. At that point, run two laps and walk one. Increase the number of laps by two each week and reduce the walking recovery time.

Once you can run 16-20 laps of the sports ground your body will be becoming conditioned for jogging on roads, in parklands and on slopes. Start on a small run for about one mile and then gradually build the distance up by 20 per cent each week. You'll be surprised by the distance you can build up to within 10 weeks.

Progressive running eFx

The progression from jogging to running requires more speed, higher exertion levels, stronger leg and torso strength and more rhythm. There are some simple drills that can help, which include walking lunges, running with high knees touching your hands and then running with high kickbacks. You can do these over 20 yards/50 metres both forwards and backwards. Start running using interval training technique:

run 500 yards/ 400 metres and then jog 500 yards/400 metres. Over a period of weeks bring your running distances up. Use the running drills as warm up and cool down exercises.

BIKE RIDING

Cycling on the spin bike can be graded up in skill in a graduated way similar to the walking program. It's also like being in the pool in that it allows you to exercise without the impact of full weight bearing. This can be great for people who have hip, knee, foot or back problems. If you're anxious about riding a bike then start with an exercise bike, progress to a 'normal' bike and next, if you are more adventurous, to riding racers and mountain bikes. Being able to get on a bike and ride safely on streets, off roads and in parks is a excellent skill which you can develop on your own or with others.

Basic bike riding eFx

There are three main types of exercise bike: upright, semi-reclined and spin bikes. These usually come with pre-set weight loss programs. However, it is a good idea to know what level to select and to be able to set a program manually. As with walking, if you are extremely obese or very obese then exercising at a light to moderate exertion level may be sufficient to lose weight. If you are obese or overweight then to lose weight you have to work at a moderate to high exertion level.

If there are no programs on the bike you can construct your own, using duration, exertion level and speed of peddling. Keep the resistance at a level that provides mild resistance. Just think of three speeds: fast, medium and slow. An example is to start at a slow pace (ie, rate of spinning) for five minutes to warm up. Over the next five minutes take the pace up to moderate for 30 seconds and back to slow for 30 seconds. For the following five minutes try moderate for 15 seconds, fast for 15 seconds, moderate for 15 seconds and then slow for 15 seconds. Then cool down at a slow pace for three minutes. The aim is to spin the pedals at a rate that challenges your exertion level.

Once you are familiar with interval training you can substitute changes in resistance for spinning speed. Choose three resistances: light, medium and hard. Try the interval program explained above, but at light,

The spin bike gets your legs spinning, your heart humming and you up and off the seat!

medium and hard resistance rather than slow, medium or fast spinning.

Semi-reclining exercise bikes are good for people who are uncomfortable and have pain riding on an upright bike. They also have a wide seat so they are much more comfortable for the butt conscious rider.

Intermediate bike riding eFx

Take your exertion up to a higher level on a spin bike. This is done by increasing the rate at which you pedal, so that your legs 'spin'. The bike is designed for you to stand and pedal; when you stand up the demands on the body increase, as you now have to do a full body exercise, using more of your upper torso to support and balance the body and to generate power for leg drive as you push and pull on the handles to counterbalance the legs.

When cycling outdoors carry a bike tire repair kit, pump, some basic tools and a container of water.

Once you feel confident about using a stationary exercise bike you can explore the world of outdoor cycling. There are many different types of bike to choose from, so look for one that suits your interest. To begin with you may want to consider a hybrid bike, which combines features of on-road and off-road bikes. It allows for a more comfortable upright sitting position whilst pedaling, but also has a frame and wheel design that's suitable for on-road cycling. To start with, try choosing a flat riding route, where as you did with stationary bike riding you can develop an interval spinning or resistance program to maintain your exertion levels.

Once you are confident with flat riding, you can choose riding routes with hills of varying gradients. Choose a route that overall works you at a moderate level of exertion.

Progressive bike riding eFx

Off-road cycling can add the X-factor to your riding program. You need an off-road mountain bike, with the appropriate tires, rims, frame, seat and pedals. The off-road experience takes you over varying surfaces such as sand, dirt, gravel, wooden bridges and mud. Begin on fire trails, and then try walking trails. Consult an off-road riding guide or cycling club to find the best route for you.

PILATES

Pilates develops your body awareness, co-ordination, flow of movement and torso dynamics. Many therapists use Pilates for exercise rehabilitation and conditioning. There are two main streams of Pilates: mat-work and studio Pilates. Mat-work Pilates requires very little equipment and therefore is the kind most commonly taught at gyms. There are also specialised Pilates studios. These studios contain Pilates equipment such as the reformer, cadillac, waunda chair and ladder barrels to support and shape the movements of your body.

In the paragraphs below we describe some Pilates mat-work exercises that will help develop your torso strength and dynamics. You can integrate these into your overall exercise program at home or the gym. Breathing technique is important in order to gain the full effect.

Basic Pilates eFx

1. The pelvic curl starts with the spine in neutral, ie with the pelvis flat and a slight arch in the lower back. Hands are placed beside the body and knees bent to 90 degrees (black shirt). Breathe out and tilt the pelvis so that the lower back 'imprints' or pushes into the floor (orange shirt). Push through the legs, reaching the knees away from the body as you feel each vertebra touch the floor to reach the final position (green shirt). Breathe in at the top of the movement. Breathe out and come down to the start position.

2. The basic chest lift and hula can be done lying down with the legs down and the hands behind the head, keeping the elbows wide. For a basic chest lift (orange shirt) start with the head on the floor. Breathe out, lifting the head up to look between the legs. As the sternum moves down and towards the pubic bone, reach the tailbone towards the heels in opposition. Take a breath in to return to the floor and a neutral spine.

The hula involves adding a small rotation to the chest lift position to the left (black shirt), returning to the centre and then rotating to the right (green shirt). If you are not very

1. The pelvic curl and movement through the spine.

2. Chest lift and hula strengthens your abdominal muscles.

3. Spinal twist with legs in a table top position progressing to straight legs.

4. Roll up in a full body movement to lengthen the spine, tone the abdominals and stretch the hamstrings.

strong you may wish to return fully to the floor between rotations. To increase the difficulty of these exercises you may lift the legs into the air in a table top position, ie with the hips and knees bent at about 90 degrees (white shirt). We suggest that you try this with your feet on a bench, wall or fit ball before you attempt it unsupported.

3. The basic spinal twist is done with the legs in a table top position, either unsupported or on a fit ball. The arms are in a T position, 90 degrees to the body. Keep the knees and feet together as you take a breath in and gently roll on the pelvis for about 30 degrees (orange and green shirts). Breathe out and return to the centre. To increase the difficulty, once you rotate to 30 degrees with the knees bent you may straighten one leg (white shirt) or both legs (black shirt); bend them in before returning to the start position.

4. Breathe in to raise the arms and breathe out to roll up through the chest lift position to sitting. Take a breath in while maintaining the C shape of the spine, then exhale to the start position.

5. Start rolling in a seated position with knees pulled to your chest and hands around the lower legs. The closer to the ankles you hold, the greater the abdominal challenge. Start with feet off the ground and lower back slightly curved (orange shirt).

As you breathe out, try and activate the deep transverse abdominal muscle by drawing the lower abdomen in towards the spine. It should be a gentle contraction and feel as though you are trying to narrow the space between the two pelvic bones. It should be soft enough to move the spine and not restrict the breath but strong enough to feel as if the spine is supported.

This abdominal movement should be sufficient to rock you off balance and into the roll. Try and keep the back curved as you roll towards the shoulder line. Breathe in and try to roll back to a balanced sitting position. To increase the challenge, roll with the legs in a frog position, holding onto the ankles with the hands. Before attempting this roll be confident that you can roll safely onto the base of your neck as the leg position increases the length of the roll.

6. Swimming is done lying face down. Lift one arm and the opposite leg up at the same time, keeping the neck elongated and reaching through the crown of the head. Hold the position of the spine as you lower the arm and leg but lift the other side. You may try doing three beats as you breathe in and three as you breathe out (green shirt).

The cobra position begins with lying face down, hands beside shoulders. With the breath in, extend up onto the elbows (orange shirt), then breathe out to extend up into the full cobra, gently assisting with the arms (black shirt). Return to the elbows with the inhalation first and then to the face down position. If you have a stiff back then try the half cobra, going only to the elbows.

Four point kneeling is a great variation for people who feel uncomfortable lying face down. You can reach through the opposite arm and leg, trying to bring them parallel to the floor (white shirt). Try six repetitions on the same combinations of leg and arm before changing over to the other arm and leg.

5. Rolling is a great way to dynamically activate the abdominal muscles and to discover how they can influence your balance.

6. Back extensions: swimming, half cobra, cobra and four point kneeling opposite arm and leg reach.

Focus on the opposition created by feeling as if you're reaching through the crown of the head in one direction and through the feet in the opposite direction.

7. Lateral strength and stability: clams, single leg reach and double leg reach.

7. This series helps to strengthen muscles required for single leg balance in the hip joint and in the torso. For clam 1 begin in a side lie position, with the hips bent to 45 degrees and knees to 90 degrees. Have both legs together and the side of the torso just off the floor. With the breath out, lift the top leg up but keep the feet touching (green shirt), then breathe in to close the legs. For clam 2 lift both feet off the ground (female white shirt). The single leg side-reach starts with both legs straight. Reach out through the top leg, lifting it up (black shirt). This can also be done with a double leg lift (male white shirt). Create opposition in the spine to prevent the side of the torso from touching the floor.

Intermediate Pilates eFx

8. Start with both legs drawn to the chest with the upper torso in a chest lift. Ensure that you slightly curl into the lower back, elongating the spine by reaching through the tailbone. For a single leg stretch, stretch one leg forward, holding the other knee to the chest. Stretch both legs forward, bringing the hands beside the body, for a double leg stretch. Stretch the legs out while breathing out and bring them in as you breathe in.

Try to maintain a light transverse abdominal contraction with the inhalation.

9. Begin with the knees drawn to the chest and reach both legs out bringing the hands beside the body with an exhalation. Breathe in and beat the arms up and down (about 15-20 degrees) five times and continue this as you breathe out. The aim is to do 100 beats of the arms in 10 breath cycles before returning to the start position.

10. Lying face down with arms out in front of the body, breathe in and reach through one arm and the opposite leg, lifting them off the ground while extending up through the spine. Breathe out and return to neutral.

CHAPTER 4 | EXERCISEFx FOR A HEALTHIER YOU | 65

8. Abdominal single and double legstretch are both dynamic abdominal exercises.

9. Hundreds: developing abdominal endurance.

10. Back extension with arm and leg lift.

11. Full body support: pike and plank.

12a. Start position for the side bend.

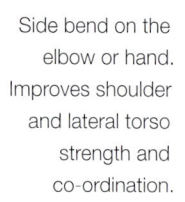

Side bend on the elbow or hand. Improves shoulder and lateral torso strength and co-ordination.

12b. Finish position for the side bend.

The pike begins from a four point kneeling position. Exhale and push through the hands, extending through the legs into an upside down V shape. Reach the heels into the ground, keeping the lower back and neck straight.

From the pike position you can straighten your body out into a plank. The challenge is to maintain the length of the spine, keep the shoulder blades flat to the back and to rotate outwards through the shoulders.

Aim to work the big knuckle of the index fingers and big toes into the mat. To increase the weight into the heels for the pike, try lifting the toes.

Progressive Pilates eFx

12. Side bend on the elbow or hand. Improves shoulder and lateral torso strength and co-ordination.

Start in a semi side lie position, with the forearm or hand on the ground. The knees are slightly bent and the foot of the top leg is in front. With an exhalation, elongate through the spine to open out into a slight arch, reaching the hand over the head. With a breath in, return to the start position.

13. Hold the plank position and then reach through one of your legs lifting it up into the air. Elongate through the leg as if someone is pulling your leg (male). To increase the challenge, do a leg pull in a back support position (female). To reach this position, start in long sitting with the hands beside the hips. Push up into a straight body position. Keep a nice straight body as you lift up one of the straight legs. In both exercises, try to keep the back of the knees long and the shoulders broad. Try to feel a sense of opposition between head and both heels.

14. Start on your back with the legs at 45 degrees, with arms to the side and upper torso in a chest lift (male). Breathe in and roll up into a V shape, bringing the hands to a parallel position. Breathe out to return to the start position.

13. The leg pull challenges your balance and develops buttocks, hamstring and abdominal strength.

14. The teaser pushes your balance to the limits.

RESCUE me | 68

1. Balanced arch.

2. Balanced arch (black) and balanced curl (blue).

3. Twist.

GYROKINESIS®

This is a form of exercise that is unique in its systematic approach to generating movements that require extension, flexion, twisting and side bending of the spine. Each of these movements is taught independently and they are then combined to make spiral movements of the body. The technique is a full body approach to exercise. As a beginner, you feel as if your body is being bombarded with new sensations as you

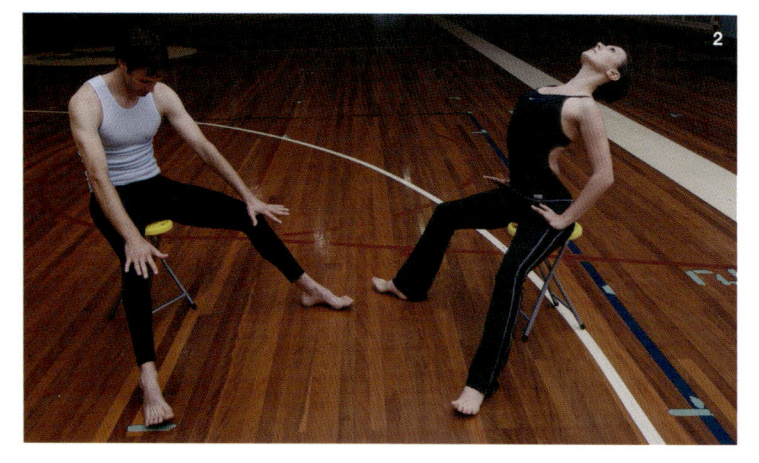

CHAPTER 4 | EXERCISEFx FOR A HEALTHIER YOU   69

create movements that start from the pelvis, spread through your body's natural lines of movement, through the joints and then to the outer extremities, reaching to the tips of the fingers and toes and the top of the head. The breath is used to help shape movements and to create a flow of movement from one position to the next. The movements develop co-ordination and strength for the many functional activities in daily life that require you to pivot and twist the body.

The exciting thing for weight loss aspirants is that in order to start Gyrokinesis practise all you need is a chair. This makes it easy to do both in the office and at home. To learn Gyrokinesis exercise method you must find an instructor who has been trained in its method.

The start position for the chair or stool exercises is sitting in a neutral upright position with legs apart, on a chair that is high enough to allow you to freely move through the pelvis. Gyrokinesis movements are the balanced arch and curl, twist, sideways arch, wave forward and reverse wave.

4. Side bend.

5a-5b.
Chest release incorporates horizontal arm circles with a twist and vertical arm circles with a side bend.

6a-6b-6c-6d.

The forward wave involves the balanced arch moving forward, changing into a curl and then returning up into a balanced curl. This can also be done in the opposite direction for the reverse wave.

RESCUE me | 70

GYROTONIC®

Gyrotonic methodology uses specifically designed equipment to support your body in fuller and more complex movements. The cobra is the main piece of equipment. It uses a pulley-tower system with weights as resistance for strengthening your stabilising and dynamic movement muscles. It also uses a handle unit designed to shape and support your body in a mixed repertoire of movements, combining flexion, extension, side bend, twisting and spiraling movements of the spine.

Through these movements you develop coordinated use of the shoulder girdle and pelvis, affecting the way you use your arms and legs and improving your ability to perform everyday functions and leisure activities, from sitting, walking, running and swimming to picking up objects (especially when you twist at the same time as bending), developing a good golf swing and skiing.

The equipment is designed for different body types and sizes and is great for all ages and cycles of life. It can be used as a stand-alone system as an aid to weight loss or integrated into cross training to improve the technique, form and flow of other exercises or activities.

3. A pregnant woman stretches her body in a forward arch. The handle units guide her direction.

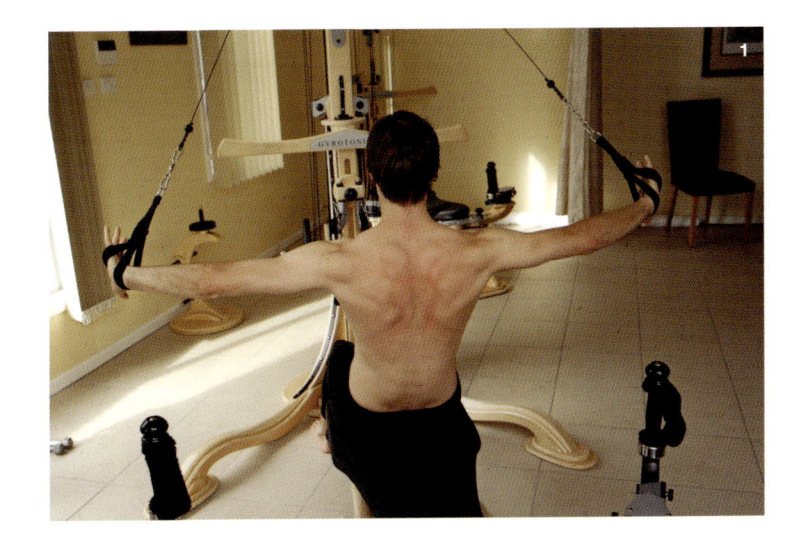

1. The pulley-tower system supports the full width of your dynamic movements allowing you to reach further.

2. The pulley-tower is used for full body, leg and abdominal conditioning.

GYM

The gym provides a safe and supportive environment in which you can develop the basic skills of lifting, pushing and pulling. There are four main types of exercise systems taught in most gyms: machine work; cable work; free weights and body weight-dependent exercises.

The advantage of working in the gym is that you can progress from using equipment that shapes your movements to more complex full body motion tasks. The exercises help you develop the strength to do everyday functional movements and you can get usable results quickly. Exercises can easily be progressively controlled through the amount of resistance, number of repetitions and the speed of the task.

Understanding proper technique with lifting, pushing or pulling will increase the full body nature and enjoyment of the exercise.

Watch out for compensatory movements like extending the spine to help lever weights up and hiking your shoulders up. Using compensatory movements is a way to determine muscle fatigue so you know when to stop. Remember, it's using the correct technique and creating the best form of movement that matters most, not the number of repetitions, the amount you lift or even the speed at which you do it.

Most gyms offer a variety of exercise classes for cardiovascular fitness and body conditioning.

The best way to lose weight is to work with lighter weights doing a higher number of repetitions (15-20), repeating the exercise two to three times. Changing the speed of the exercise is a valuable progression. Increasing the speed challenges your joint control, especially when you change the direction of the exercise, and it also increases the cardiovascular demand on the body.

Basic gym eFx

Machine work is the best way for an eFx beginner to start. Its advantage is that the movements are reproducible and simple to do. This allows you to start developing technique whilst the machine helps you to hold the form of the exercise.

Machines for the upper body include the pec deck, the seated row, seated chest press, biceps and triceps machines. Machines for the lower body include quadriceps extensor, hamstring curl, calf press and the leg press.

When on a gym program, record resistance, repetitions, speed, sets and machine settings.

1. The quadriceps machine develops quadriceps leg strength to straighten the knee. This can be good for activities such as the movement from sitting to standing or kicking a ball. The hamstring machine develops knee bending strength which can help you with running, particularly as you swing the leg.

2. The leg press machine is the all-rounder. It nicely combines the hip, knee and ankle joints. The benefits will be felt with the sit to stand movement, lifting, pushing and pulling.

Intermediate gym eFx

Cable work or exercising using pulley machines increases the challenge for you to maintain joint control. The cable system allows your joints to move in their own natural way while the resistance, from a set pivot point (the pulley), provides direction and support of the movement you are training.

Upper body cable exercises include triceps pulls and latissimus dorsi or 'lat' pull downs.

3. The triceps pull improves your ability to keep the shoulder blades in a set position and strengthen the abdominal muscles as you push down through your arms. It involves setting the body with the knees bent and a straight spine on a slight forward incline. Keep the elbows to the side to work on setting the shoulder blades into a fixed position as you extend the elbows while pulling the cable down.

1. Quadriceps leg extensor machine and (top of picture) hamstring curl machine.

2. The split pedal leg press machine challenges both legs to make them work equally as hard.

3. Triceps pull can help develop awareness of setting the shoulder blades into a stable position.

4. Lat pull downs challenge your ability to control your shoulder blade movements when reaching above your head.

4. The lat pull down is a good exercise to feel how the shoulder blade moves across the back as you raise and lower your arms. It is done in a seated position with the spine straight. Hold the handles with your hands wide apart and on the downward slope of the bar.

Start with the bar in front of the face at nose height. Slowly raise the bar, trying to keep the elbows wide allowing the shoulder blades to open out wide. Feel the shoulder blades rotate upwards as you raise your arms. Don't let the shoulder blades hike up around the ears. Once the arms are at full length, gather the shoulder blades together to pull the bar down. Feel the downward rotation and the inward glide of the shoulder blades. Keep working the outward movement of the elbows to prevent bunching of the shoulder joint.

There is now a wide range of towers in the gym with a split pulley system. With these systems you may even be able to adjust the position of the pulley. Using the split pulleys in a high position you can do standing chest press, standing flyes and standing pull downs. Using the split pulleys on a low setting you can do squat lifts. With a single pulley set in a low position you are able to do upright rows and leg pulls (if you have the appropriate leg strap) exercises, some of which are described below.

Progressive gym eFx

Free weights are barbell or dumbbell exercises. They are more complex than machine work because they require you to control the direction of the movement, which involves dynamic stability and co-ordination of the joints. The advantage of free weight exercises is that they make us stronger for movements that we tend to do often in our everyday lives. For the upper body, barbell exercises are a great starting point with free weights. Because barbell exercises require you to use two arms together for the one movement, you have considerable control. Dumbbell exercises are more difficult. As you hold a separate dumbbell in each hand, more control and precision of movement from each arm is needed, across a greater range of motion.

5. Chest press. Start by lying on the bench. Legs may be beside the bench or on top of it. The main thing is to keep the spine in a neutral and relaxed position. Hands should

be wide on the bar. Breathe in and lower the bar down to the nipple line, working the elbows outwards and feeling the shoulder blades come together.

When the bar is near or just touching the chest, the elbow and wrist of each arm are close to vertically aligned. Avoid arching the lower back as you lower the bar. Have someone stand behind your head ready to assist you to lift the bar or guide it back onto the rack.

6. Upright rows. Space legs hip width apart, either together or in a small lunge with one foot in front. Start with arms straight and hands shoulder width apart. With a breath out draw the bar up to chest height, drawing the elbows apart and feeling the shoulder blades coming closer together. Return to the start position and breathe out.

Military Press. Legs are hip width apart, either together or in a small lunge. Hands are shoulder width apart. Lift the bar to the shoulders for the start position. Now push through the arms to lift the bar up slightly in front of the body while breathing out. Avoid overarching the lower back as you lift. Return to the shoulder height as you breathe in.

With all upper body barbell exercises, how far apart you place your hands can be varied to increase the challenge of the exercise. Be aware that when the hands change position the form of the exercise will also change.

5. Bench (Chest) press.

6. Upright row and military press. Both exercises can be done with a normal bar or with a 'w' bar that reduces the strain on the wrists.

7. Bicep curls.

7. Bicep curls. These can be done with both arms moving together with dumbbells or a barbell or in opposite directions with dumbbells. You may do them in standing or sitting. Keep the elbows to the side of the body and the shoulder blades set throughout the exercise. Breathe out and bend or curl through the elbow to lift the weight to shoulder height.

8. Dumbbell flyes. Always start conservatively, using light weights. Lie on the bench with feet besides the bench. Start with the dumbbells touching above the chest with the arms extended and a slight bend in the elbow. Breathe in and open out through the arms as if they are wings. Only lower the weights to the level of your body on the bench. Breathe out and bring the arms together again.

For the lower body, barbell squats and lunges require more control than when using dumbbells. For these barbell exercises the bar balances across the shoulders or chest which act as a fulcrum point. If you do the lift unevenly or get off balance the bar may tip, potentially causing you to lose control of the exercise.

Practise these in an exercise rack before attempting to lift the weight freely. Also, have someone nearby to watch that you stay balanced.

9. Squats. Commence standing up with feet wide apart, keeping the heels down. Use a wide hand grip, with the bar resting on the shoulders just above the shoulder blades. As you squat focus the weight into the heels, keeping your feet and knees in alignment so that they point in the same direction. Flex into the hips, keeping a straight back. The torso will incline forwards as you go down. As you push up, exhale and work through the heels and the hips to keep legs and torso correctly aligned as they return to the upright position.

10. Lunges. Stand with one foot forward and the other a good stride length behind. The front foot is flat and the rear foot can be on its toes. Start with both legs straight and a square pelvis. Bend the front and back knees so your torso goes vertically down. The challenge is to do a vertical drop, trying not to let the torso lean forward. To do this you may have to adjust the distance between your feet. Exhale to push up though the legs and return to the start position.

11. Body weight exercises. These can be the hardest of all the exercises in the gym. To do them correctly, without compensatory movements, you need to be well conditioned and well coordinated. Free body exercises include chin ups, dips, push ups, abdominal and back extensions, dynamic step ups and fit-ball exercises.

8. Flyes require a high degree of control through the shoulders.

9. Squats in the rack keeping you safe. Get someone to watch your technique to help you perform the lift correctly.

10. Lunges using the rack to provide balance for the bar so you can focus on technique and form.

1. Start with something simple and fun - repeated punching with straight jabbing.

2. A successful hook leaves a good smile on your face.

BOXING

Boxing will get the heart pumping and help shed the weight. It can be a simple way to get started on cardiovascular exercise if you're not suited to running or aerobic classes. You can start at a very basic level doing arm work only, and as you become more interested you can develop technique focusing on leg movements to generate a variety of punches. Skipping develops hand-foot co-ordination, leg strength and speed. With increasing fitness and improved reflexes and footwork you can develop basic combinations, learn to bob and weave and deflect basic punches. From here you can progress to shadow boxing, and sparring.

Boxercise can provide hours of fun - the problem is stopping once you're 'hooked'. Most gyms offer classes or you can take the personal trainer option.

Make sure you like the person holding the mitts. Aim for the centre of the mitts and try to make the hits brisk and sharp. It is the change of direction and accuracy that develops the power and strength of your arms.

Basic boxing eFx

1. Learn to hit. Start with repeated straight jabbing or upper cuts. Stand in a boxing stance, with your feet hip width apart and one foot forward. If you're right-handed put

the left foot forward; left-handed, right foot forward. For straight repeated jabs (overs), start with both hands at chin height and then punch straight with one hand and then quickly with the next into the focus mitts. You hit into the opposite focus mitt such that your right hand contacts the trainer's right focus mitt. For repeated upper cuts (unders) you start with your gloves at waist height and then hit alternatively upwards into the opposite focus mitt. The trainer holds the focus mitts facing towards the ground at abdominal height. Try hitting straight overs for 30 seconds then change to uppercut unders for 30 seconds. Or count out 30 hits and then change. You can repeat this for five minutes. Try varying the pace of hitting: slow, medium and fast.

Intermediate boxing eFx

There are four boxing hits: straight jabs with the leading hand, straight punches with your dominant back hand, upper cuts and hooks. Your boxing stance for all four remains the same, but bring the front arm up to about cheek level and the back hand to chin level. After a hit, try and return as quickly as possible to this position.

Straight jabs are short and sharp punches from the front hand. Straight punches require the same sharp movement from the rear hand but more power can be generated if you rotate through the pelvis as if you slightly step into the punch by pushing off the back leg.

Upper cuts are low body punches with a bent elbow aiming for the abdomen (mitts must be held low). They are similar to a bicep curl.

2. Hooks are a great punch though if done poorly you can get off balance very quickly. The main aspect to consider is pivoting through the foot, keeping the elbow high and not over-reaching. Pivoting the foot allows you to move the pelvis through the line of the punch. When you perform a hook with the front arm pivot on the front foot, as if you are squashing a bug on the ground. If the hook comes from the rear hand, then pivot on the rear foot. Remember to recover feet and hands back to your boxing stance.

It is recommended that you use inners or wraps or bandages in your gloves, as they support the bones in the wrists and hands.

Skipping builds fast feet to adapt to changes in body position. It seems simple but jumping rope requires good co-ordination. It's best to start with double leg jumps;

3. It's obvious that you are having fun when you start learning about the art of deflecting punches.

try to 'stay on your toes' between jumps. Progress to jumping from one foot to the other as if running. Then try jumping with one foot slightly in front of the other. Once you can do this you can come up with a variety of combinations. The most important thing with skipping is to keep doing it. Double skipping is for the advanced skipper and requires a high degree of timing and practise.

Progressive boxing eFx

Once you have learnt a few different combinations and your footwork is secure and reproducible, you are ready to begin sparring with your friend the mitt holder. Start with sequences that the mitt holder calls out. You have to respond quickly and always recover your feet and glove position before you do the next sequence. Try to move around: backwards, forwards, sideways and in circles. Begin with bouts of one minute, and aim to build up to five minutes.

By the time you've worked up to five minute bouts, you will have developed the endurance and the alertness required for defensive moves. At this point you can add in jabs from the mitt holder so you're required to deflect the punch. To improve your anticipation of punches, learn to be a mitt holder. When holding the mitts keep your hands and elbows soft.

If you don't have a partner, you can practise combinations and footwork using boxing bags of various sizes. Speed balls help develop rhythm. If you don't have access to a punching bag, then try shadow boxing which involves doing your punching combinations in the air. It's a good idea to do this in front of a mirror so you can see your own technique. You'll be surprised by how quickly your arms fatigue and your heart rate goes up.

Boxing is an art, and like dancing it requires rhythm, timing and form. Keep relaxed, try and stay balanced and don't over reach.

DANCE

Music combined with physical movement that has intention, expression, rhythm, technique and form creates something wonderful, and that is dance.

Dance is an inheritance that we can all share and express across and within cultures and eras. When you play a song with a good rhythm, at the right volume, before you know it your foot is tapping and arms are swinging. The urge to move to music is hardwired into us. Think of infants or toddlers spontaneously dancing to a song, their legs bending and their hands clapping. We all know it's good for us.

One of the amazing things about dancing is that once you're really going you can nearly lose yourself in it, not even realising how much you've exerted yourself. When the music asks you to keep moving, somehow you manage to find that little bit more energy and expression. When you are on a dance floor the real winner is the person with intention and a smile so it doesn't matter if

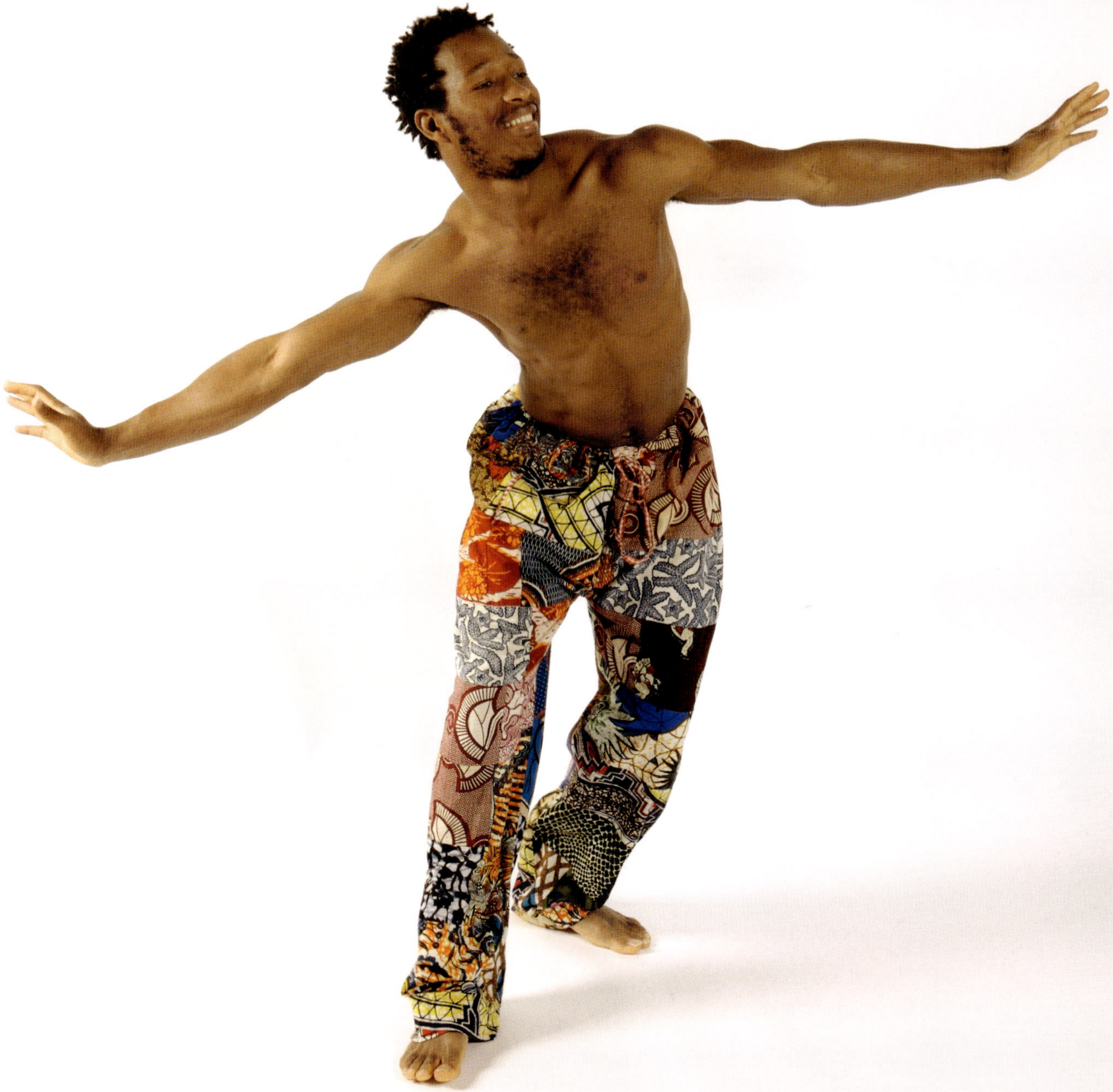

you feel a bit uncoordinated or shy - just move with the intention of having fun.

Dance breaks down barriers and gives people the opportunity to express themselves. Salsa dancing, for instance, is not just about learning about steps and turns. It's also about dancing with other people, learning how different people move and responding to dancing cues. Even dance styles that seem to celebrate the individual, like ballet, African or contemporary, are in fact very much team driven. Dancing, leaping, spinning, bending, swinging, gliding, clapping, stepping, twisting, bopping, rapping, tapping and moving together is what it's all about. There is a step there for everyone; it's just a matter of finding it.

The best thing for the basic mover is to begin; for the intermediate mover it's to keep going and for the progressive mover it's to never stop learning.

WINTER SPORTS

If you live in regions where it snows regularly, make the best of the opportunity and strap some skis or a board under your feet. Being in the snow, riding the lifts, skiing or snowboarding down runs are all exciting ways to burn energy. Skiing or snowboarding can feel a little awkward to begin with but with the right guidance you can be up and moving very quickly.

These activities require full body control and good ability to weight shift, rotate through the body, squat - and, when you begin, being prepared to fall, laugh at yourself, get back up and have another go. For the new beginner, lessons are worth their weight in gold. You can move quickly from snowplows to the next place to slide to a stop. Then comes parallel skiing where you angle the skis downhill using ski poles and the slope of the run to help shape turns and control your speed. It is an exhilarating experience.

EXERCISE IS EVERYWHERE

Housework activities that you do once or twice a week can fit just fine into your eFx plan. Energy may be expended very well through everyday activities such as vacuuming the house, mowing the lawn, managing the garden, washing the car, hanging the clothes on the line, pushing a shopping trolley, or bathing the kids. Park your car some distance from your destination to give yourself an extra walk. Take the stairs and walk the long way around to keep the body moving.

Take the extra step and get involved in a team or club activity. It provides social opportunities and there is normally a level or sport that everyone can be involved in. Determine your role in the team and learn the rules. It is a great way to share skills and experiences. For the basic eFx get involved, intermediate eFx play a contributing role and for progressive eFx be competitive.

Bend it to shape it. Move it or lose it. Go back to the mirror and take another look and plan your rescue.

Chapter 5
The Rescue Me Flavour Diet

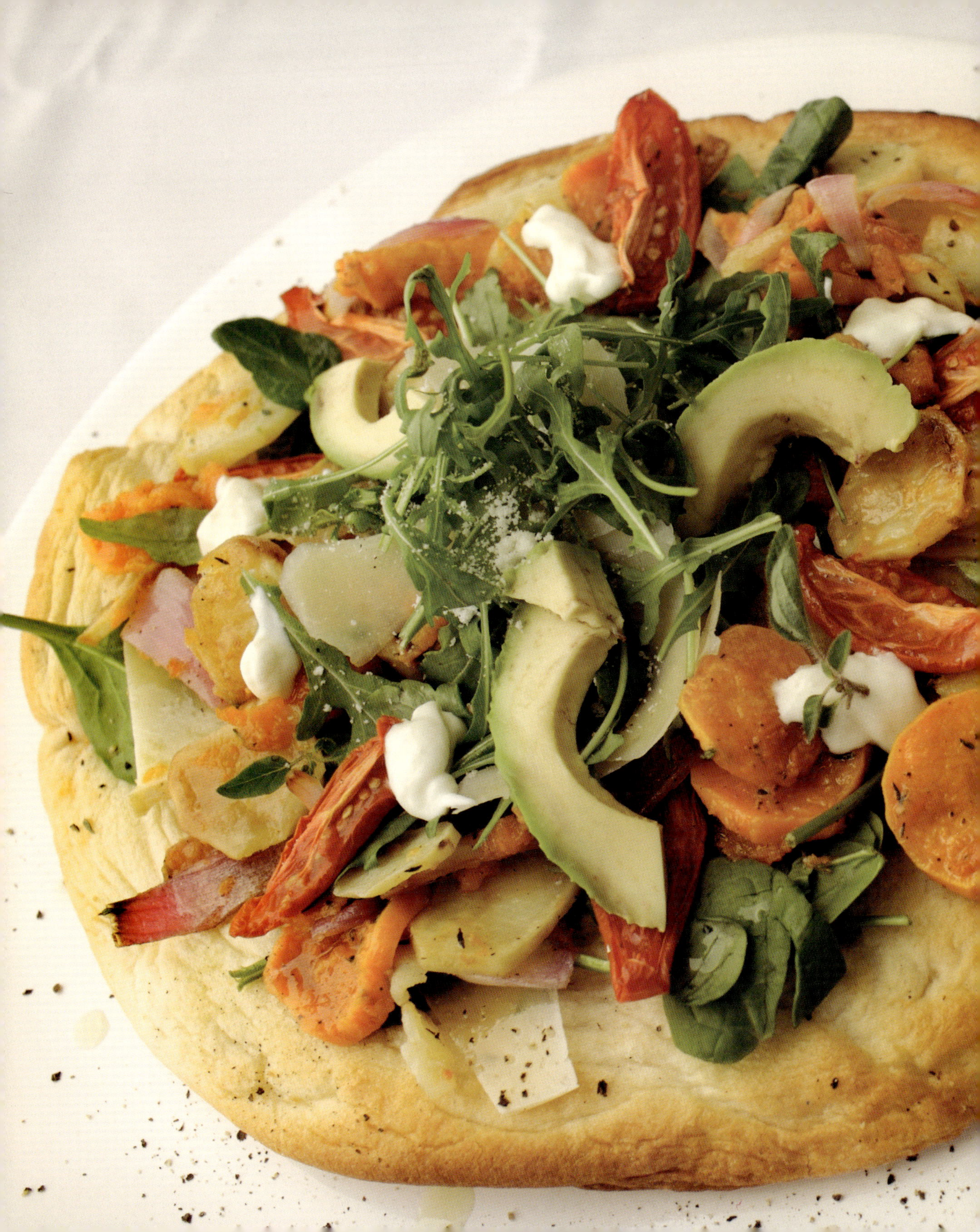

Chapter 5: The Rescue Me Flavour Diet

It's time now to get ready to prepare your own foods rather than having takeaway, rushed meals on the run or a stand-up meal in the kitchen. Look forward to shopping for new ingredients to stock your pantry and planning some new meals. Gradually you will become independent in the kitchen and increase your enjoyment of mealtime as you learn to appreciate taste and flavour as never before.

Give up on the old cooking style and adopt a new approach aimed at a new result. In the first few weeks of this plan we will not suggest that you cook every meal, every day. Take your time to change, by integrating our meals with some of your own, and you will be more likely to succeed with the Rescue Me plan. In this way you'll learn the system correctly and stick to it for life, because you are tutoring yourself with our guidelines, you're learning as you go and you're changing your habits slowly and forever. Prepare for week one early. A suggested pantry list is on page 86, so check your current pantry and go shopping in preparation for the commencement of your new Flavour Diet. As part of your overall plan, make your kitchen a more interesting place. Bring in some fresh flowers and decorate the room with some fresh herbs.

Combine this 12 week Flavour Diet with your exercise program and the results will be exciting and long-term. If you are an experienced cook then start at week 5 or 6.

If you don't prepare and cook more than a meal or so a week, then please start the Flavour Diet at week 1. The choice of plates and bowls will assist you with your portion control. During the first 10 weeks of the plan why not serve the meals onto smaller plates and, where appropriate, into bowls rather than dinner dishes. During weeks 11 and 12 why not go 'gourmet' with some reverse psychology: choose the largest dinner plates you have and place the small serving in the middle of the plate, confirming your success with portion control.

Pizzas do not need heaps of cheese and sauce. Go with the tasty healthy look.

RESCUE me

STAGE ONE | COOKING TO EAT | WEEKS 1-5

Pantry list

Replenish these as you run out
Extra virgin olive oil
Balsamic vinegar
Soy sauce
Barbecue sauce
Cranberry sauce
Breakfast cereal
Vegemite
Honey
Jam
Peanut butter
Seeded mustard
Eggs
Cheese for grating
Butter
Pepper (black peppercorns and cracked pepper)
Sea salt
Stock powder or cubes
Bay leaves
Dried oregano
Cans of diced tomatoes
Dry spaghetti
Penne pasta
Long grain (basmati) rice
White sugar
All-purpose flour
Garlic
Ginger (fresh)
Chilis (fresh)
Onions (brown & white)
Potatoes
Carrots
Lemons

Wooden stirring spoons
Set of fridge-ware plastic containers

Instructions for preparation of new meals this week are included in text.

Week 1: A gentle start

If you are a new cook, get started with a few new items in the kitchen. A set of wooden stirring spoons, some fridge-ware plastic containers, a new kitchen apron, some good quality kitchen knives, a metal wok and wok stand if cooking with electricity and a few pots of fresh herbs at the kitchen door. This week you only need to prepare three meals.
Take it slowly and you'll achieve your goals.

	BREAKFAST	LUNCH	DINNER
MONDAY	CEREAL Hi-fibre *NEW*	YOUR CHOICE	YOUR CHOICE
TUESDAY	YOUR CHOICE	YOUR CHOICE	PASTA Napolitana & Salad *NEW*
WEDNESDAY	YOUR CHOICE	YOUR CHOICE	YOUR CHOICE
THURSDAY	CEREAL Hi-fibre	YOUR CHOICE	GRILL Lamb Chops Rice & Vegetables *NEW*
FRIDAY	YOUR CHOICE	YOUR CHOICE	YOUR CHOICE
SATURDAY	YOUR CHOICE	YOUR CHOICE	YOUR CHOICE
SUNDAY	YOUR CHOICE	YOUR CHOICE	YOUR CHOICE

Week 1

CHAPTER 5 | THE RESCUE ME FLAVOUR DIET

Monday

BREAKFAST | CEREAL | Hi-fibre

Prepare any favourite cereal that has at least a hint of 'healthy' about it, milk and a small amount of sugar plus any piece of fresh fruit. Tea or coffee to suit your taste.

Tuesday

DINNER | PASTA | Napolitana & Salad

Twenty minutes before you want to eat, boil enough pasta for the meal and heat the jar of Napolitana in a small saucepan. Strain the pasta and serve it in your favourite bowls. Pour sauce over, add some grated cheese (any kind will do) and a grind of pepper to finish it off. Serve with salad.

Thursday

DINNER | GRILL | Lamb Chops, Rice & Vegetables

Choose lean meat and trim off the fat. Cook the meat your favourite way. Prepare some green vegetables and boiled rice (prepare according to packet instructions). Pepper, salt and mustard will improve the taste of the lamb. Enjoy a glass of red wine if you choose. A piece of fresh fruit after dinner will finish the meal.

You've prepared four meals this week. Well done. Look again at your exercise plan and have a happy healthy weekend.

Shopping list

Milk
Grainy bread
Fruit
Napolitana sauce
Salad greens
Green vegetables
Lamb chops
Red wine

Red wine is said to be good for the health of your heart and research shows that white wine improves lung function better than any other form of alcohol. We will be suggesting that you enjoy wine with some of your meals, but always in moderation: two standard glasses of wine per day for men and one per day for women.

TIPS OF THE WEEK

Drink more water every day.

Choose more interesting, grainy, tasty bread.

Shopping list

Bread
Milk
Fruit
Salad greens
Tomatoes
Cold meat slices
Canned beets
Chutney
Ground beef
Lamb chops

Week 2: Increasing the pace a little

By now you will be looking for ways to improve your pantry and pick up pace with your shopping. Buy in plenty of fresh salad items. Choose the lamb chops with the least fat and trim them when you get them home ready for the weekend grill. Don't buy too much bread as this is one item we will be suggesting you slowly cut down on soon. Buy canned beets for now, but in a few weeks you'll be cooking your own.

Instructions for preparation of new meals this week are included in text. Blue Cells indicate meals that are repeats from previous weeks.

REPEAT MEAL

NEW MEAL *NEW*

	BREAKFAST	LUNCH	DINNER
MONDAY	CEREAL Hi-fibre	YOUR CHOICE	YOUR CHOICE
TUESDAY	YOUR CHOICE	BREAD Salad Roll *NEW*	YOUR CHOICE
WEDNESDAY	CEREAL Hi-fibre	YOUR CHOICE	PASTA Spaghetti Bolognaise *NEW*
THURSDAY	CEREAL Hi-fibre	YOUR CHOICE	YOUR CHOICE
FRIDAY	YOUR CHOICE	YOUR CHOICE	YOUR CHOICE
SATURDAY	YOUR CHOICE	YOUR CHOICE	GRILL Chops & Tomatoes
SUNDAY	YOUR CHOICE	YOUR CHOICE	YOUR CHOICE

Week 2

CHAPTER 5 | THE RESCUE ME FLAVOUR DIET

Tuesday

LUNCH | BREAD | Salad Roll

You can make this as big as you like. One or two rolls but keep them healthy! Tomato, canned beets, onion and any salad greens you like, plus put in a bit of grated cheese or cold meat and some chutney. Have a juice or a piece of fruit with it and you will feel invigorated for the rest of the afternoon.

Wednesday

DINNER | PASTA | Spaghetti Bolognaise

This old favourite takes a little time but is well worth the effort. Cook up an onion and a clove of garlic in a large saucepan in a small quantity of olive oil. Add ground beef, a cup of beef stock made from a stock cube, a pinch of dried oregano and a can of crushed tomatoes. Stir and cook for 30 minutes. Add pepper and salt to taste. Cook the spaghetti in plenty of boiling water, drain and pour the meat sauce over it. Add a small amount of grated cheese.

TIP OF THE WEEK

Buy nice tasty cheese for the topping on the pasta to increase the flavour.

Shopping list

Bread
Milk
Yoghurt
Cheese
Fruit (apples, pears, berries)
Cantaloupe (rockmelon)
Salad greens
Tomatoes
Canned beets
Cucumber
Green vegetables
Stir fry vegetables (bell pepper, shallots, snowpeas, bok choy)
Curry sauce
Asian-style noodles
Whole cooked chicken
Cold meat slices
Chicken or beef for stir fry
Chevapi skinless sausages
Red or white wine

Instructions for preparation of new meals this week are included in text. Blue Cells indicate meals that are repeats from previous weeks.

REPEAT MEAL

NEW MEAL

Week 3: Learn to stir fry

Because you will be cooking stir fry this week and this style of cooking will become important to you you will need to buy a wok. You'll find one in the Chinese quarter in your city or in any kitchen appliance store. High heat over gas is the best stir fry method. If you have electricity then you will need a wok stand to go over the element. Eating stir fry meals with chopsticks is a great idea as it usually slows down your eating.

	BREAKFAST	LUNCH	DINNER
MONDAY	CEREAL Hi-fibre & Fresh Fruit	YOUR CHOICE	YOUR CHOICE
TUESDAY	BREAD Toasted with Condiments or Tomato (NEW)	YOUR CHOICE	RICE Curry Chicken & Boiled Rice (NEW)
WEDNESDAY	BREAD Toasted with Condiments or Tomato	BREAD Salad & Cold Meat Sandwich	YOUR CHOICE
THURSDAY	YOUR CHOICE	YOUR CHOICE	STIR FRY Vegetables & Chicken or Beef Strips (NEW)
FRIDAY	FRUIT Fruit Salad (NEW)	YOUR CHOICE	YOUR CHOICE
SATURDAY	YOUR CHOICE	STIR FRY Noodles with Vegetables	YOUR CHOICE
SUNDAY	YOUR CHOICE	YOUR CHOICE	BARBECUE Chevapi sausages & Salad (NEW)

Week 3

Tuesday

BREAKFAST | BREAD | Toasted with Condiments or Tomato

Two pieces of bread. No butter but your favourite condiment - peanut butter and jelly (small quantity), cheese, honey or vegemite. Or try adding some grilled tomatoes and cracked pepper instead of condiments.

DINNER | RICE | Curry Chicken & Boiled Rice

Pull cooked chicken into pieces. Heat a jar of curry chicken sauce and pour over the chicken. Place in ovenproof dish and put in oven heated to 320°F/180°C. Boil rice according to packet instructions and throw in a knob of ginger to add extra flavour to the rice. Don't over-eat and balance two thirds rice to one third chicken. Follow the meal with a piece of fresh seasonal fruit and a cup of tea.

Thursday

DINNER | STIR FRY | Vegetables & Chicken or Beef Strips

Trim and slice fresh meat. Chop and prepare all vegetables. Heat the wok until sizzling. Pour in a little oil and light soy sauce. Pan fry the meat strips separately and set aside. To keep the flavour balance correct and avoid turning the stir fry into a stew with one common flavour, cook the aromatics (shallots, onions, ginger, chili and garlic) in the main wok first and set aside for a few minutes. Steam the vegetables (bell pepper, snowpeas and bok choy) in a fresh saucepan then add the meat and the vegetables into the mix in the wok, adding a small amount of stock to keep the meal juicy. Heat up high and stir all ingredients together for one minute then serve immediately.

Friday

BREAKFAST | FRUIT SALAD | Fresh Seasonal Fruits

Choose pears and apples where you can - buy them fresh and in season. Fresh berries and cantaloupe are also great if they are locally produced. Chop fruit and squeeze a little lemon juice over. Add a small serve of yoghurt. Tea with low fat milk and no sugar to follow.

Sunday

DINNER | BARBECUE | Chevapi Skinless Sausages

Celebrate the end of the week with a trip to the supermarket for the healthiest sausages on the planet. Chevapis are very low in fat and easy to cook. Heat up the barbecue, pour half a glass of red wine for the cook, and prepare your favourite salad. Don't over-cook the meat - serve it with barbecue sauce and mild seed mustard plus the other half a glass of wine!

Note of interest: The amount of fat listed on the label is the content before the meat is cooked. After cooking this content will be considerably less, depending on the cooking method used.

TIP OF THE WEEK

Buy in some good bottled juices for your breakfast and drink water water water during the day.

Curing the new wok. All new cast-iron pots and skillets have a protective coating on them that must be removed. American companies use a special food-safe wax; imports are covered with water-soluble shellac. In either case, scrub the item with a scouring pad, using soap and the hottest tap water you can stand. Then rinse and dry completely. NOTE: Never soak or let soapy water sit in the pan for any length of time. Apply a thin coat of melted, plain vegetable oil to the entire surface, both inside and out. Cooking oil or sprays should not be used for seasoning because they'll eventually make the surface sticky. (Both, however, can be used for cooking.) Coat the handle, edges and corners of the pan, and if it has a cast-iron lid, coat that, too. Wipe out excess shortening with a paper towel.

Preheat your oven to 350°F/180°C. Line the lower oven rack with aluminum foil to catch any drips. Place the cast iron pot upside-down on the middle rack and bake for two hours.

Turn the oven off and let the pan cool before removing it from the oven. Wipe again with a paper towel. Once seasoned, a new, natural-finish pan will acquire a brownish-gray colour. With time and use, and re-seasoning, it will become shiny and black. Seasoning is an ongoing process, and a well-seasoned pot has a surface that will release food easily. A rule of thumb: if the crust on your fried fish or chicken begins to stick and burn, it's time to re-season.

Shopping list

Bread
Milk
Yoghurt
Ricotta or cottage cheese
Eggs
Fruit (include apples, pears)
Salad greens
Tomatoes
Stir fry vegetables
Salad vegetables (red onions, cucumber, bell pepper)
Flat leaf parsley
Other fresh herbs
Broccoli
Peas
Asian-style noodles
Cold meat slices
Ground beef
Beef for stir fry
Cooked chicken
Fruit juice (include apple juice)
White wine

Instructions for preparation of new meals this week are included in text. Blue Cells indicate meals that are repeats from previous weeks.

| REPEAT MEAL |
| NEW MEAL NEW |

Week 4: Portion control, portion control, portion control

Three dinners to cook this week and 11 meals to prepare in total. Keep your portions small and add extra fruit or salad to meals if you need more. Make a mixture of one dessertspoon of yoghurt to a cup of apple juice and use this on your cereal instead of milk. It's sweet and healthy. Eat whatever you like on the weekend, but keep it lean and sensible in line with your new eating and cooking style and your exercise program.

	BREAKFAST	LUNCH	DINNER
MONDAY	CEREAL With a glass of juice	BREAD Salad Sandwich	PASTA Spaghetti Bolognaise
TUESDAY	CEREAL	BREAD Cold Cuts & Salad Sandwich	YOUR CHOICE
WEDNESDAY	BREAD Toast & Grilled Tomatoes	YOUR CHOICE	STIR FRY Vegetables, Beef & Noodles
THURSDAY	CEREAL	YOUR CHOICE	YOUR CHOICE
FRIDAY	FRUIT Fruit Salad	SALAD Garden Salad NEW	YOUR CHOICE
SATURDAY	YOUR CHOICE	YOUR CHOICE	GRAIN Chicken & Fried Rice NEW
SUNDAY	YOUR CHOICE	YOUR CHOICE	YOUR CHOICE

Week 4

Saturday

DINNER | GRAIN | Chicken & Fried Rice

Boil up some basmati rice the night before. Make a thin omelet by mixing one egg per person and cook in an oiled skillet until set. Chop omelet and set aside. Stir fry diced fresh vegetables including broccoli and green peas. Mix all together with the cooked chicken pieces and the rice. Season with light soy and black pepper. Stir until hot and serve in bowls with chopsticks and a glass of white wine.

Broccoli is cousin to the cauliflower and cabbage. It is rich in vitamin C and glucosinolates and has a powerful action in the detoxification process in the liver. It is loaded with carotene, which assists with immunity and is especially beneficial for protecting the eyes against sunlight damage and age-related macular degeneration. Steam it or stir fry it but don't overcook it. It's at its best when a little crunchy.

Friday

LUNCH | SALAD | Garden Salad

Buy fresh, seasonal, locally grown produce (where possible). Use lettuce, tomato, cucumber, red onion, bell pepper, parsley, chili and any other fresh produce that catches your eye. Buy organic if you are near an organic market. Wash it. Store it in the fridge. Throw it out when it's old. Make a simple dressing in a jar of 3 parts olive oil and 1 part lemon juice, cracked pepper and fresh herbs. Use some of the dressing and store the rest in the fridge for later.

TIP OF THE WEEK

Search for berries of any kind to add to fruit salad or fresh fruit drinks.

Drink water water water during the day.

Thursday

BREAKFAST | CEREAL | Raw Muesli

Make up a dry mix of oatmeal, pinenuts, almonds, sunflower seeds and chopped dried fruit. Add in some bran and a crushed-up handful of your previously favourite cereal. Use apple juice and a small amount of yoghurt instead of milk as the liquid. Oatmeal is a remarkably versatile grain with many health benefits. As well as being a good source of carbohydrates it is high in soluble fibre. Which may help to lower cholesterol. It is an ideal breakfast food, especially in winter.

LUNCH | SALAD | Greek Salad

In a bowl mix together diced tomatoes, red bell pepper, cucumber, red onion, black olives, cubes of feta cheese and torn flat leaf parsley. Add lemon juice vinaigrette with a pinch of oregano, slices of soft garlic and cracked pepper.

Friday

DINNER | PIZZA | Tomato-based with Cheese, Pepperoni & Olives

Buy pizza base and prepare topping. Use a bottle of Napolitana as a base sauce. Cover with grated cheese (mozzarella is best), lean

Week 5

sliced meat and black olives. Bake in oven at 420°F/200°C until crisp and crusty. Throw a handful of fresh arugula, a few sprigs of fresh oregano and some torn basil on top - avocado will make it even better. Drizzle balsamic vinaigrette (3 parts oil, 1 part balsamic vinegar) over and enjoy with a glass of red wine. Depending on your exercise program and your desired weight loss, note the number of slices you consume and plan to reduce that next time you prepare this meal.

Saturday

BREAKFAST | GRAIN | Pancakes with Honey or Lemon Juice

220g/7oz plain flour, 60g/2oz butter, 1 cup milk, 2 eggs and a pinch of salt. Put flour into a bowl and make a well in the middle. Gently heat butter, milk and salt together. Break eggs into the well and slowly mix, adding the liquid as you go. Whisk until the consistency of thin cream. Heat a buttered skillet and gently pour the batter in. When the edges lift turn the pancake. Practise makes perfect with pancakes. They are worth it. Squeeze over a little lemon juice. Adding a few slices of banana and a little honey will satisfy the sweet tooth. Keep the serving size small.

DINNER | ROAST | Chicken & Vegetables

Rub a fresh chicken all over with a mixture of lemon juice, rosemary pieces and olive oil. Place 2 half lemons and a bunch of rosemary into the cavity and tie the legs together with cooking string. Season with a little salt and a grind of black pepper. Bake at 350°F/180°C. Cut your favourite root vegetables into small pieces and put them in the baking dish. Cook for 1 hour or until cooked to your liking. If you are in a hurry, cut the chicken into two halves, lay cavity side down in the hot pan and surround with vegetables. Exclude potatoes from this meal and add steamed broccoli. After you steam the broccoli, quickly toss it in a hot skillet with a little olive oil and some creamed garlic (see Tips). Remember quantity control and enjoy the flavour of a small serving. Reserve some of the chicken for Monday's lunch.

Soups with homemade stocks are interesting and nutritious. They can start with a braise or simply with meat bones and vegetables. Add a clove or two of garlic, cumin, bay leaf, celery and fresh chili and use your imagination to create the base for wonderful meals. Use the stocks for risottos, stews and a range of soups. Don't add excessive salt - let the ingredients convey the flavours. A splash of wine just before serving will give that little boost to the flavour that makes the meal special.

TIPS OF THE WEEK

Gently fry a clove of garlic with its husk on until the centre is soft. Use this as a creamy addition to a meal when garlic is required.

Add unsalted almonds and raisins to your cereal to make the taste more interesting.

Buy green tea and make this with breakfasts and lunches.

RESCUE me

STAGE TWO | COOKING FOR TASTE | WEEKS 6-9

Shopping list

Multigrain bread
Bread for wraps (tortilla)
Pumpernickel bread
Low fat milk
Yoghurt
Feta cheese
Low fat cottage cheese
Eggs
Fruit (include pears, peaches, apples for baking)
Apples, beets, celery for juicing
Oranges
Salad greens
Tomatoes
Fava beans or similar in season
Arugula (rocket)
Flat leaf parsley
Coriander
Rosemary
Vegetables for roasting
Broccoli
Snowpeas
Olives
Couscous
Can of chickpeas
Labna (lebanese yoghurt cheese)
Falafel
Ham
Ground beef
Chicken pieces
Lamb chops
Whole chicken for roasting
Fish fillets
Chicken for stir fry
Cranberry or orange juice
White wine

Week 6: Get going with juice

Poached fruit for breakfast was a staple item in author Judith Kennedy's weight loss program. Make a few servings at a time and store in fridge containers. Poached fruit is great after coming home from the pool or from a fitness walk when you are actively losing weight. If the workout has been strenuous add a little low fat cottage cheese and a few almonds. Your new pantry list is featured this week.

	BREAKFAST	LUNCH	DINNER
MONDAY	CEREAL Muesli Fresh Fruit Salad Fresh Juice	BREAD Chicken Wrap with Salad & Chutney *NEW*	PASTA Spaghetti Bolognaise & Garden Salad
TUESDAY	FRUIT Poached Peaches or Pears Vegetable Juice *NEW*	BREAD Pumpernickel Sandwich with Feta Cheese and Olives	GRILL Chicken & Couscous *NEW* ➡ to Wednesday Lunch
WEDNESDAY	FRUIT Poached Peaches or Pears	BREAD Chickpea, Couscous, Labna & Falafel Wrap *NEW*	RICE Lamb Chops with Brown Rice *NEW* ➡ to Thursday Lunch
THURSDAY	BREAD Toasted with Condiments Fresh Juice	BREAD Lamb & Salad Sandwich	YOUR CHOICE
FRIDAY	YOUR CHOICE	YOUR CHOICE	YOUR CHOICE
SATURDAY	BRUNCH Shout yourself breakfast at the local cafe		ROAST Lemon Chicken & Vegetables *NEW* ➡ to Sunday Dinner
SUNDAY	EGGS Scrambled Fresh Vegetable Juice *NEW*	SEAFOOD Grilled Fish Fillets & Salad	STIR FRY	DESSERT Chicken & Snow Peas Baked Apples *NEW*

Week 6

Monday

LUNCH | BREAD | Chicken Wrap. Salad & Chutney

Use the leftovers from Saturday's dinner. Slice the meat finely and layer it on the wrap bread with a little fresh arugula (rocket) or parsley, a teaspoon of chutney and a grind of black pepper for a tasty lunch.

Tuesday

BREAKFAST | FRUIT | Poached Peaches or Pears with a glass of vegetable juice

Poached peaches or pears (in season) poached in cranberry or orange juice. Place halved pears or peaches in the juice and poach for 5 minutes with a few black peppercorns. Add a pinch of salt to bring out the flavour. Serve with a little yoghurt.

DINNER | GRILL | Chicken Pieces with Couscous

Marinate chicken in a mixture of olive oil, fresh coriander and garlic pieces for 30 minutes. Stir fry sliced onions, thinly sliced carrots, a drained can of chickpeas, fava beans and a pinch of cumin in olive oil. Prepare the couscous as per the packet. Grill the chicken until juicy. Mix vegetables into the couscous and serve the chicken on top. If using fresh fava beans make sure you remove the second skin from the bean - only then are you tasting the bean at its best.

Pantry list

Light olive oil
Sweet soy sauce
Light soy sauce
Fish sauce
Oyster sauce
Red wine vinegar
White vinegar
Rice wine
Hoisin sauce
Verjuice
Dried fruits:
apricots, raisins
Dried herbs and spices:
basil, turmeric, sage,
dried chili flakes,
chili powder,
cinnamon, nutmeg
Nuts and seeds:
almonds, walnuts,
pinenuts, sunflower
seeds, sesame seeds
Oatmeal
Brown rice
Short grain (risotto) rice
Brown sugar

Aluminum foil
Plastic containers

Fresh juices now become important to your dietary intake. Buy a citrus squeezer or an electric juicer. Be warned that too much fruit juice can be counterproductive as your sugar intake will go up. Use the juicer for vegetables such as beetroot, carrot, celery and a little apple.

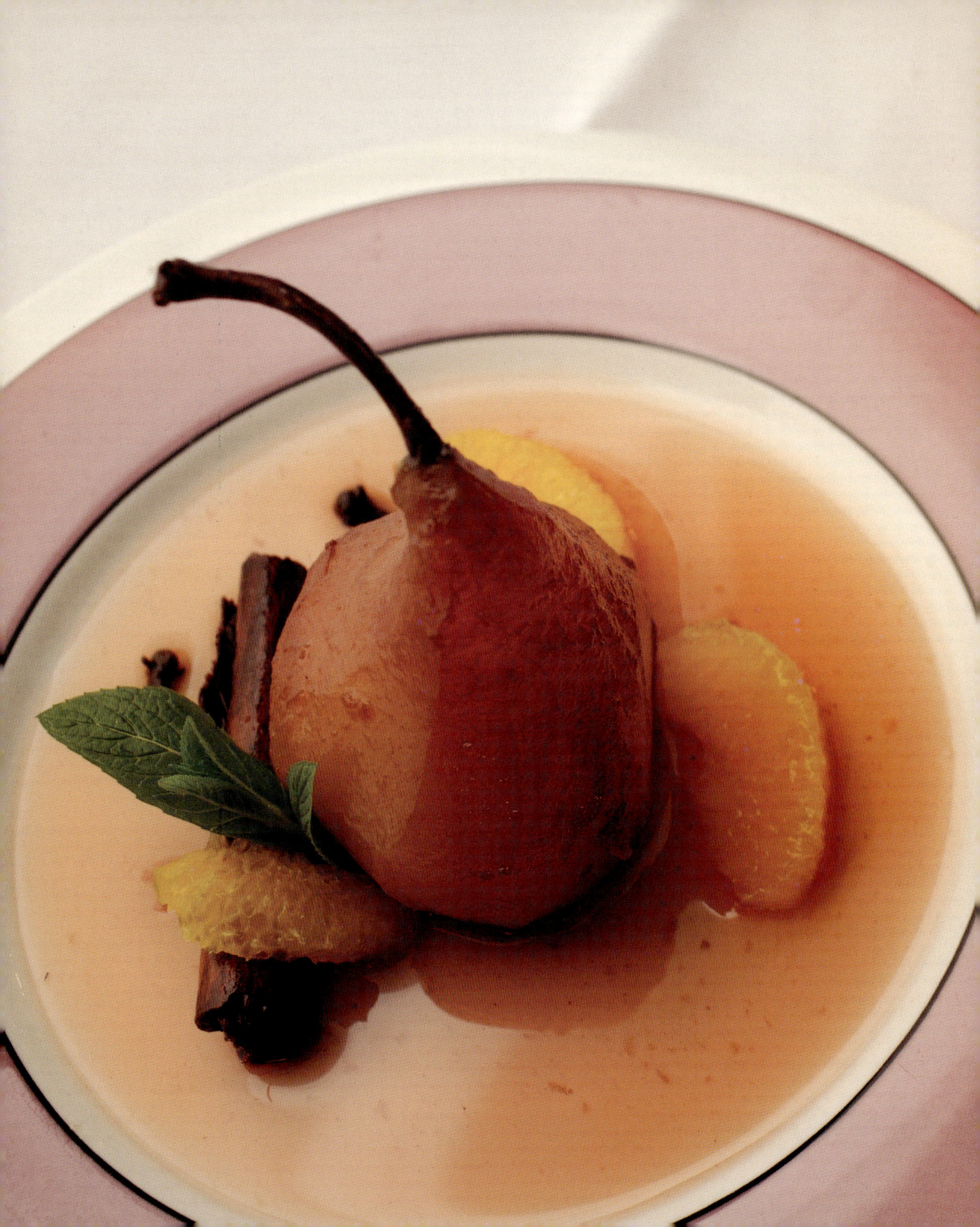

Week 6

Wednesday

LUNCH | BREAD | Chickpea, Couscous, Labna & Falafel Wrap

Another merged meal. Buy some falafel from the Lebanese takeaway. Mix the remainders of last night's meal together with the falafel, a labna (see tips) and a squeeze of lemon juice. Layer the mixture onto a tortilla wrap. Cover with mixed salad leaves and chopped tomato and fold. One wrap with a fruit juice plus a piece of fresh fruit is a very suitable lunch on this program.

DINNER | RICE | Lamb Chops with Brown Rice

Marinate chops in a combination of sweet soy (kecap manis), rice wine, grated ginger and crushed garlic for 20 minutes. Prepare brown rice as per instructions. Grill chops on medium heat to your liking. Serve rice with the chops. Dress with fresh coriander and any fresh salad. Remember to chew the meat well. Take your time and enjoy the flavour of the ginger and coriander, which give a sweet Asian tang to the taste. Save a chop for tomorrow's lunch.

Saturday

DINNER | ROAST | Lemon Chicken & Vegetables

Rub half a lemon over the chicken prior to baking. Place lemon halves in the baking dish to enhance the flavour.
Cook extra chicken for tomorrow night.

Sunday

BREAKFAST | EGGS | Scrambled Eggs & Fresh Vegetable Juice

Crack 2 eggs per person into a bowl. Add milk (30% of the volume) and mix. Pour into a pan and stir until cooked but still moist. Serve on wholegrain toast - no butter.

DINNER | STIR FRY | Chicken & Snowpeas; Baked Apples

Quick and easy. Enjoy a glass of chardonnay or sauvignon blanc with it. See Thursday week 3 for method. To make the apples: core 1 per person. Fill cavity with raisins and chopped nuts. Place in baking dish. Drizzle a little honey and fresh orange juice over. Cover with foil and bake at 350°F/180°C for 20 minutes. Remove the foil and bake a further 10 minutes to caramelise the apple. Sprinkle with cinnamon and serve.

TIPS OF THE WEEK

Labna are Lebanese yoghurt cheese balls packaged in oil in sealed jars, available from delis.

Remember quantity control and enjoy the flavour of a small serving.

Shopping list

Bread
French bread stick
Low fat milk
Yoghurt
Parmesan cheese
Ricotta cheese
Eggs
Pears
Rhubarb
Apples
Bananas
Salad greens
Tomatoes
Rocket
Celery
Cabbage
Mushrooms
Flat leaf parsley
Mint
Rosemary
Green vegetables
Can of white beans
Can of kidney beans
Can of borlotti beans
Olives
Napolitana sauce
Pizza base
Ham or other meat slices
Chicken bones
Smoked Salmon
Fish fillets
Leg of lamb
Whole chicken for roasting
Apple or orange juice
White wine
Red wine

Week 7: Now we're cooking!

Learn to make risotto this week. When planning your own meals you can be very creative and add any cooked vegetables to this famous dish. Adding cooked beet or pumpkin makes a colourful and tasty variation. Cold risotto can also make a terrific lunch on a hot day. Try it rolled in lettuce leaves with a good grind of black pepper.

	BREAKFAST	LUNCH	DINNER
MONDAY	FRUIT Fruit Salad & Yoghurt Fresh Lemon Tea *NEW*	BREAD Lemon Chicken & Salad Sandwich	SOUP Minestrone *NEW*
TUESDAY	CEREAL with Fresh Fruit	SALAD Arugula & Pear *NEW* ➡ to Wednesday Lunch	RICE Mushroom Risotto *NEW*
WEDNESDAY	FRUIT Rhubarb & Apple Stewed in Apple or Orange Juice	BREAD Lox (Smoked Salmon), Arugula & Pear Salad	GRILL Fish Fillets, Boiled Potatoes & Salad
THURSDAY	YOUR CHOICE	BREAD Sandwich with Cold Cuts Yoghurt	YOUR CHOICE
FRIDAY	FRUIT With Juice or Tea	YOUR CHOICE	SOUP Chicken Vegetable Broth
SATURDAY	GRAIN Pancakes with Honey or Lemon Juice	YOUR CHOICE	ROAST Baked Leg of Lamb *NEW*
SUNDAY	EGGS Poached in Verjuice on French Bread *NEW*	PIZZA Pizza & Salad	ROAST Lemon Chicken & Vegetables ➡ to Monday Lunch

Week 7

Monday

BREAKFAST | FRUIT | Fruit Salad & Yoghurt, with Fresh Lemon Tea

To make the tea: squeeze the lemon halves into your hand, catching the seeds. Drop one half of the lemon into the cup with the juice and pour boiling water over to fill the cup.

DINNER | SOUP | Minestrone

Chop and combine 1 onion, 1 stick of celery and 1 clove of garlic and brown in a deep pan stirring with a splash of olive oil. Add a good pinch of dried basil and sage. Pour in 1 pint of any stock. Add in 1 diced carrot and tin of tomatoes and bring to the boil. Add tinned beans and half a chopped cabbage. Simmer for 20 minutes. Add a handful of pasta and boil until the pasta is soft. Salt and pepper to taste.

Tuesday

LUNCH | SALAD | Rocket, Pear & Pinenut Salad

Thinly slice fresh pears and marinate in a small amount of lemon juice - just enough to coat the pieces. Place sesame seeds and pinenuts in a skillet and gently toast until light brown. Mix pears, seeds and nuts through arugula leaves and heap onto plates. Drizzle balsamic dressing over for a further burst of flavour.

DINNER | RICE | Mushroom Risotto

Heat leftover chicken broth or homemade stock in a small saucepan and put on very low heat on the stovetop. Sauté a handful of chopped white onion and a little olive oil in a heavy pan next to the stock. Tip in a cup of risotto rice and stir until coated with oil. Pour over 1 cup of white wine and stir for 2-3 minutes. Ladle hot stock into the rice mixture, stirring and cooking until the rice is lightly cooked (al dente). You really can't leave the stove until the rice is cooked. The addition of the stock and the stirring must be fairly continuous. Add in chopped mushrooms, grated parmesan cheese and cracked pepper. Continue cooking until mushrooms are semi soft. Serve with a sprinkling of fresh chopped parsley and a parmesan cookie (see Tips). The crunchy texture of the cookie balances beautifully with the smoothness of the rice.

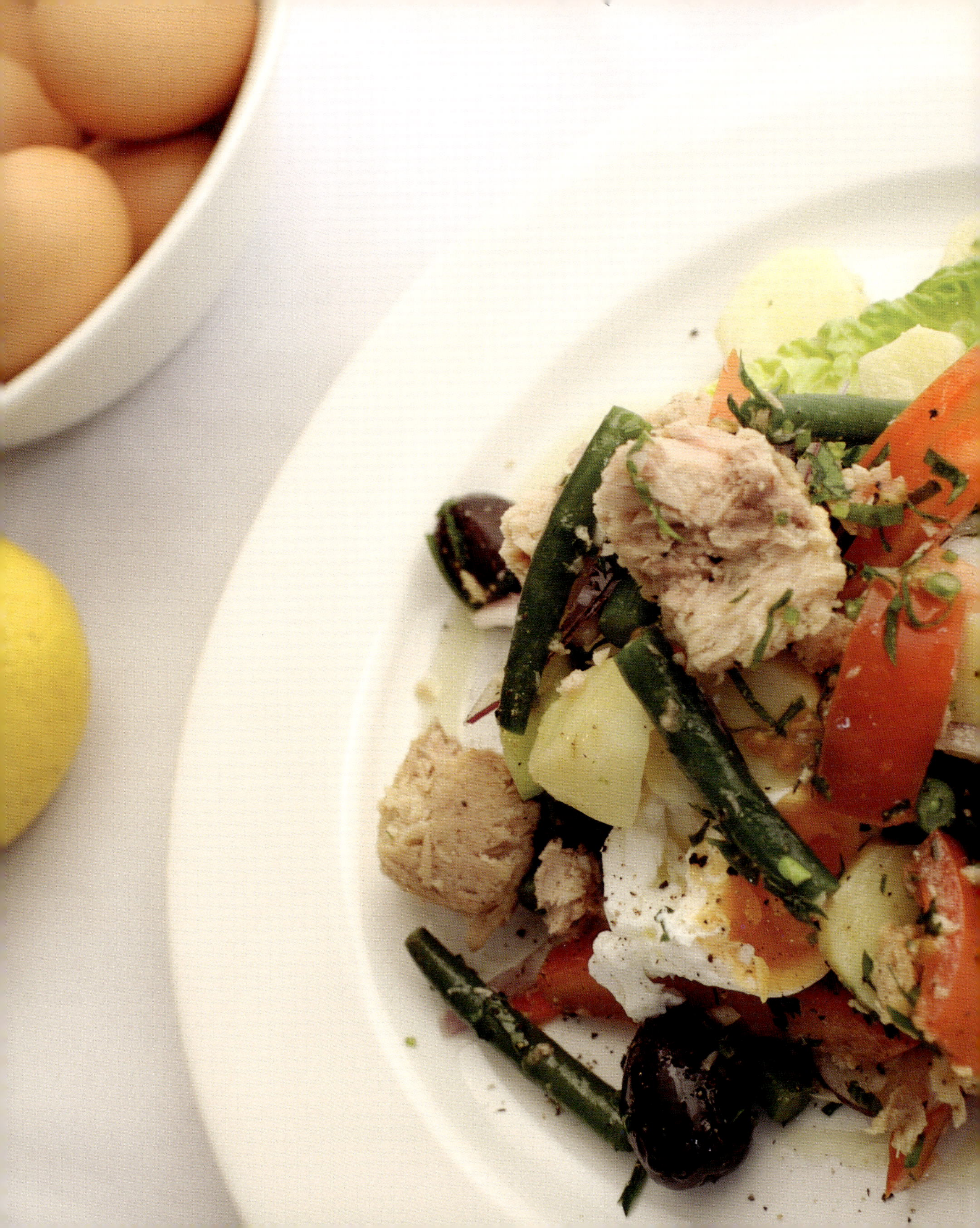

Saturday

DINNER | ROAST | Baked Leg of Lamb

Make a mixture of seeded mustard and chopped rosemary leaves. Rub all over the lamb using your hands. Sharpen some rosemary stems and spear into the lamb for added flavour. Bake at 210°F/120°C for about 2 hours per 1lb/500g. Slow-cooked lamb results in less liquid loss and a larger roast to serve. Remove from pan and carve - there's no need to let the meat sit. Boil 1 potato per person, blanch some green vegetables and toss them lightly in a pan with creamed garlic and a little oil. The umami flavour (rich, powerful taste) is a great experience enhanced by the special rosemary overtone. The mustard balances the rosemary and the hearty flavour of the lamb - a glass of red wine (if you choose) adds to the flavour feast.

Sunday

BREAKFAST | EGGS | Eggs & Tomatoes Poached in Verjuice on French Bread

This is a French provincial idea that will become a favourite. Pour a total of 1 cup (half verjuice and half water) of liquid into a skillet and bring to a simmer. Add tomatoes halved (1 per person). Cook 2-3 minutes. Add egg(s) and poach until your liking. Lightly toast a small amount of French stick cut lengthways. Place tomatoes and egg onto the toast and pour remaining reduced liquid over. Add cracked black pepper.
No fat - all taste.

TIPS OF THE WEEK

To make parmesan cookies: grate the cheese and form into a cookie shape on baking paper. Bake in a moderately hot oven until brown. Cool.

Stew some fruit in orange juice and keep in the fridge for breakfasts. Don't add sugar, just a pinch of salt to bring out the flavour of the fruit.

Make a salad for lunch at every opportunity. Tomato, lettuce, onion and chopped basil at home or for the office.

Week 8: Great taste!

Several new cooking ideas are introduced this week. A great soup, a fabulous pudding and one of the best breakfast ideas you will find. You are now developing better appreciation for the taste and texture of foods. Wine in moderation is a good way to expand the flavours of a well-cooked meal.

Shopping list

Bread
Bread for wraps
Low fat milk
Low fat yoghurt
Haloumi cheese
Eggs
Pears or peaches
Fruit for stewing
Apples for baking
Mixed berries (fresh or frozen)
Limes
Salad greens
Tomatoes, baby tomatoes
Pumpkin
Broccolini
Asparagus
Red onions
Mushrooms
Broccoli
Flat leaf parsley
Coriander
Mint
Basil
Rosemary
Bean sprouts
Rice noodles
Rice paper
Vermicelli noodles
Crushed nuts
Lamb chops
Chicken thighs
Cold meat slices
Steak
Ground beef
Fish fillets, shrimps and octopus
Cooked shrimps
Ham or chorizo sausage
Racks of lamb
Cranberry juice

	BREAKFAST	LUNCH	DINNER
MONDAY	FRUIT Poached Peaches or Pears Fresh Lemon Tea	BREAD Chicken, Salad & Cheese Sandwich	RICE Honey Lamb Chops with Brown Rice (NEW) ➡ to Tuesday Lunch
TUESDAY	CEREAL Raw Muesli Fruit Juice or Lemon Tea	SALAD Lamb Chop, Salad with Lime Juice & Olive Oil Dressing	GRILL Marinated Chicken Thighs (NEW)
WEDNESDAY	BREAD Toast & Grilled Tomatoes or Mushrooms	SALAD Sliced Cold Meat with Salad	GRILL	DESSERT Steak, Broccolini & Pumpkin Summer Berry Pudding (NEW) ➡ to Thursday Lunch
THURSDAY	EGGS Poached (NEW)	BREAD Steak & Salad Wrap	SOUP Mushroom (NEW)
FRIDAY	FRUIT Poached Peaches or Pears Lemon Tea	SOUP Vegetable	GRILL Ground Beef Burgers Haloumi Cheese & Salad
SATURDAY	CEREAL Cooked Oatmeal & Stewed Fruit (NEW)	BARBECUE Fish Fillets, Shrimp, Octopus & Baked Beets	STIR FRY Rice Noodles, Mushrooms & Broccoli (NEW)
SUNDAY	EGGS Royal Breakfast Bake (NEW)	PASTA	SEAFOOD Vietnamese Rice Paper Rolls with Vermicelli & Shrimps (NEW)	ROAST	DESSERT Rack of Lamb & Tomato Salsa Baked Apples (NEW) ➡ to Monday Lunch

Week 8

Monday

DINNER | RICE | Honey Lamb Chops with Brown Rice

Boil 1 cup of rice to 2 cups of water. This will make 4 cups of cooked rice. Throw a knob of ginger into the water when cooking for a little extra flavour. The grains should be cooked through yet still a little nutty in the centre. Brush the lamb chops with a 50/50 mixture of honey and light soy sauce. Grill the cutlets to your taste and serve on a bed of rice. Leave some lamb for lunch tomorrow.

Tuesday

DINNER | GRILL | Marinated Chicken Thighs

Make a marinade mixture of 50/50 oyster and fish sauces. Toss the chicken pieces through the sauce until well coated. Grill the meat to your taste, turning frequently, and serve with a green salad.

Wednesday

DINNER | GRILL | Steak, Broccolini & Pumpkin

Peel and chop the pumpkin. Mix together a good pinch of nutmeg, sea salt, pepper, softened garlic and balsamic vinegar. Rub mixture all over the pumpkin. Bake in a moderate (350°F/180°C) oven for 30 minutes or until brown. Blanch the broccolini and serve the vegetables with grilled steak. Cook an extra piece of steak and refrigerate ready for tomorrow's lunch.

While the vegetables are cooking, start to prepare the pudding.

DESSERT | Summer Berry Pudding

You need: stale bread, cranberry juice, brown sugar, mixed berries. Boil juice and lightly sweeten with a little sugar. Add mixed berries and poach for a few minutes. Cool. Remove crusts from the bread and soak the slices in the juices for a few seconds. Arrange bread in layers in serving bowl and pour fruit over. Enjoy with a spoonful of low fat yoghurt and remember, a small portion is all you need.

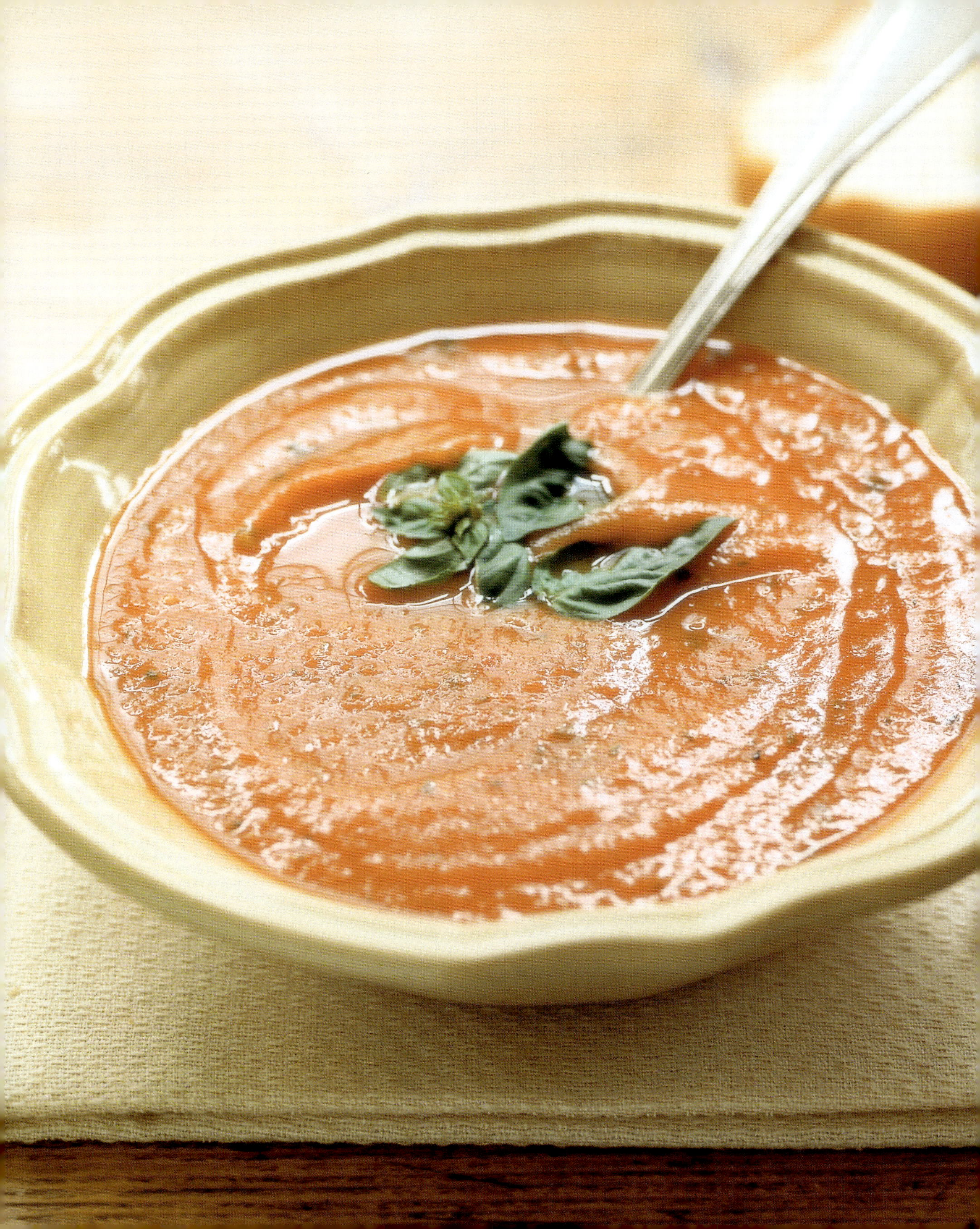

Week 8

Thursday

BREAKFAST | EGGS | Poached
Poach the egg to your liking and throw on a generous amount of chopped parsley and a grind of black pepper. If aiming for weight loss, skip the toast and have two eggs. Vegetable juice or tea.

DINNER | SOUP | Mushroom or Pumpkin
Sauté one medium sized chopped brown onion in a little olive oil with a grind of black pepper and a pinch of grated ginger. Slice 8oz/240g mushrooms and stir into the onion mix until cooked through. Add 2 cups of vegetable stock and simmer for 20 minutes. Blend with half a cup of skim milk and serve with a small spoonful of plain yoghurt and a sprinkle of fresh chopped parsley. Cracked black pepper will always bring out a richer mushroom flavour. Follow the soup with fresh fruit, a few almonds and green tea.
Substitute 1 cup of cooked pumpkin for mushrooms, if that is your preference.

Saturday

BREAKFAST | CEREAL | Cooked Oatmeal & Stewed Fruit
Measure $\frac{1}{2}$ a small cup of oatmeal per person. Soak overnight in 1 cup of water and a pinch of salt. In the morning add a splash of milk and bring to the boil while stirring constantly until thickened. Add a small quantity of fruit that has been stewed in natural fruit juice.

DINNER | STIR FRY | Rice Noodles, Mushrooms and Broccoli
Boil noodles for 5-8 minutes in water with a pinch of sea salt. Strain and top with sautéed mushrooms and steamed broccoli. Wonderful as a side dish with seafood or as a main.
An alternative method is to gently stir the cooked noodles with a little oil on the stove top and add the seafood. Fold together. Grind a little black pepper over and serve immediately.

Sunday

BREAKFAST | EGGS | Royal Breakfast Bake

Per person: 1 egg, 1 slice grain bread, ½ brown onion, 6 baby tomatoes, grated tasty cheese, ½ cup milk plus pancetta ham, olive oil and red wine vinegar. Drizzle oil and vinegar over onion wedges and stir fry on the stovetop until caramelised. Spread half of the onions into a small baking dish. Lightly butter bread both sides and lay over the onions, tilting one edge of the bread upwards to encourage browning of the crust. Whisk eggs and milk together and pour over bread. Sprinkle remaining onion, grated cheese and shredded ham or chorizo on top. Toss baby tomatoes on top and cook at 350°F/180°C for 20-25 minutes until brown. To protect the custard-like egg mix, place the baking dish into a larger oven-proof dish and pour in enough very hot water to reach half way up the side of the baking dish. Sprinkle a little more balsamic vinegar over the tomatoes. Just before serving throw some chopped flat leaf parsley over and a grind of black pepper. This dish is suitable for the whole family, however use less balsamic for the children. Why not coffee (no cream) today?

LUNCH | PASTA/SEAFOOD | Vietnamese Rice Paper Rolls with Vermicelli & Shrimps

Boil vermicelli for 2 minutes in hot water with a pinch of salt. Drain well. Prepare cooked shrimps, a chopped boiled egg, fresh coriander, fresh mint and bean sprouts. Dip rice paper into boiling water. Lay on a warm plate. Cover half of the paper with prawn mix, mint and noodles. Fold into cigar shapes. Serve with a dipping sauce made up of hoisin sauce, crushed nuts, fresh chili and lemon juice. Enjoy! Have 2 or 3 of these as they have a low GI and low fat content.

Week 8

CHAPTER 5 | THE RESCUE ME FLAVOUR DIET

DINNER | ROAST | **Rack of Lamb & Tomato Salsa; Baked Apples** to follow
Rub the lamb all over with chopped rosemary and olive oil. Slow roast in a baking dish until done to taste. Chop tomato, fresh basil and rosemary and toss in a small amount of olive oil and lemon juice. Season to taste. Garnish the lamb with the salsa and a sprig of fresh watercress. Cook extra lamb for tomorrow. Follow with baked apples.

Baked beetroot is hard to beat! Wash it, don't cut the tails off and wrap in aluminum foil. Place in a baking dish and slow bake until tender. Depending on the size of the vegetable it may take several hours to cook through. Zapping in the microwave for 5 minutes first can speed up the process. Remove the skin and cut into pieces after it's cooked. Lightly cover with a little lemon juice and virgin olive oil. Serve hot or cold. Use this in your risotto and slice some into your next salad, as they will keep in the refrigerator for some time.

TIPS OF THE WEEK
If you feel like having a glass of wine, match reds to big tasty foods and whites to less complex foods.

Have a small slice of crunchy toast with the soup for extra texture.

Keep drinking fresh vegetable juice or lemon tea after breakfast.

Shopping list

Bread
Pumpernickel bread
Low fat milk
Yoghurt
Ricotta cheese
Feta cheese
Eggs
Fruit for stewing
Oranges
Red and green apples
Berries for smoothie
Salad greens
(include cos lettuce)
Tomatoes
Asparagus
Watercress
Beets
English spinach
Mushrooms
Flat leaf parsley
Dill
Snowpeas
Red onion
Red bell pepper
Cucumber
Cauliflower
Leek
Braise vegetables:
turnips, rutabaga (swede),
pumpkin
Celery
Sweet potato
Zucchini
Avocado
Arugula
Smoked eggplant dip
Olives
Agar agar
Linguine pasta
Pizza base
Cold meat slices
Pork and lamb fillets
Fresh shrimps
Chops or steak
Lamb pieces for soup
Chicken bones for stock
Rosé and white wine

Week 9: Portion, portion, portion

This week we introduce you to braising. This is a stovetop or oven method of cooking, which results in a remarkable exchange of flavours between the liquid and the solids. We also introduce you to the concept of getting your hands into the food. Clean hands can mix food better than any implement. Practise makes perfect.

	BREAKFAST	LUNCH	DINNER
MONDAY	FRUIT Fruit Salad & Yoghurt Fresh Lemon Tea	BREAD Pumpernickel Sandwich with Lamb	GRILL Pork Fillets & Apple Sauce with Asparagus *NEW* → to Tuesday Lunch
TUESDAY	CEREAL Cooked Oatmeal & Stewed Fruit	SALAD Meat Slices & Greens	SALAD Lamb Fillet with Watercress & Yoghurt *NEW* → to Wednesday Lunch
WEDNESDAY	EGGS Omelet with Sautéed Mushrooms *NEW*	BREAD Pumpernickel Sandwich with Lamb	GRILL | DESSERT Linguine & Shrimps Apple Delight *NEW*
THURSDAY	FRUIT Fruit Salad & Yoghurt	SALAD Mixed Garden Leaves & Tomato Fresh Juice	GRILL Chops or Steak & Vegetables
FRIDAY	EGGS Poached with Tomatoes in Verjuice	SALAD Greek Salad	SOUP Lamb & Vegetable
SATURDAY	EGGS Scrambled with Grilled Tomatoes	SOUP Cauliflower with Truffle Oil *NEW*	BRAISE Turnips, Carrots, Pumpkin and Rutabaga with Grilled Steak *NEW*
SUNDAY	FRUIT Smoothie *NEW*	SALAD Waldorf *NEW*	PIZZA | DESSERT Vegetarian Agar Agar *NEW*

Week 9

Monday

DINNER | GRILL | Pork Fillets & Apple Sauce with Asparagus

Marinate pork for 30 minutes in light soy sauce. Peel and core apples (1 per person). Cut into wedges and simmer in small saucepan with 1 tablespoon white vinegar and 1 teaspoon brown sugar. Stir until liquid is sauce consistency. Grill meat. Steam asparagus. Spoon sauce over fillets. Reserve some apple sauce for Wednesday night's dessert.

Tuesday

DINNER | SALAD | Lamb Fillet with Watercress & Yoghurt

Stir fry strips of lamb in a little oil. Mix them into a bowl of trimmed watercress, lettuce and English spinach, tomato slices, onion rings and low fat yoghurt. Mix and turn with your hands until all the meat is covered with yoghurt then heap onto a bed of greens. A grind of black pepper and a glass of Rosé will complete the experience.

Wednesday

BREAKFAST | EGGS | Omelet with Sautéed Mushrooms

Slice and sauté mushrooms (or tomatoes and onions). Set aside. Roughly beat two eggs and ½ a cup of milk per person. Pour into hot (not too hot) buttered frying pan. Gently lift sides and cook until nearly set. Pile mushrooms onto one side of the omelet and sprinkle a little grated cheese over. Grill until gently brown and the egg is set but not overdone. Add black pepper to taste. Turn half of the omelet onto the piled mushroom side and serve. Chopped parsley adds to the taste. Note: if the egg mixture is still a little juicy and fluffy, you have done a great job! Add one small piece of grain toast.

DINNER | PASTA | Linguine & Shrimps

Drain the cooked linguine (1 handful per person). Stir fry garlic, lemon zest and a little fresh chili in olive oil until fragrant. Add in peeled shrimps and a squeeze of lemon juice. Add 1 cup of white wine (preferably chardonnay) and a handful of chopped asparagus. Stir for a minute. Serve over hot linguine and add another squeeze of lemon juice. A sprinkle of fresh dill will just top it off.

DESSERT | Apple Delight

Add a small amount of brown sugar to the apple sauce remaining from Monday night. Heat through or serve cold. Top with a spoonful of ricotta cheese.

Saturday

LUNCH | SOUP | Cauliflower with Truffle Oil

To serve 2. In a large pot lightly stir fry 1 tablespoon olive oil, 1 diced onion, 1 sliced leek, 1 diced potato and ½ a medium cauliflower cut into pieces. Add 2 bay leaves, then 2 cups of chicken stock. Gently boil for 30 minutes. Remove bay leaves and puree the soup. Season with lemon juice, sea salt and fresh black pepper. Serve in wide soup bowls. Drizzle a few drops of truffle oil over as you serve it.

DINNER | BRAISE | Turnips, Carrots, Pumpkin & Rutabaga with Grilled Steak

Peel and cut vegetables into quarters lengthways and place in an oiled baking dish. Toss in a mixture of sea salt, pepper and softened creamy garlic. Partly cover with a mixture of half water, half red wine (cabernet is a good choice) and bake, covered at 350°F/180°C for 45 minutes or until the vegetables are tender. Transfer the baking dish to the stovetop and boil briskly until the liquid reduces, shaking the pan frequently until the vegetables are coated with a sticky sauce. Just before serving, add another splash of red wine that will enhance the taste further. The transfer of flavour from vegetable to sauce and from sauce to vegetable is both intriguing and flavoursome. Serve with a lean piece of grilled steak and some greens. A glass of cabernet works very well here!

Sunday

BREAKFAST | FRUIT | Smoothie
Blend fresh fruit and low fat milk. Add ice cubes in summer

LUNCH | SALAD | Waldorf
This only takes 10 minutes to prepare. You need apples cut into bite-sized chunks, sliced celery, orange segments, toasted walnuts, cos lettuce leaves and a small amount of plain yoghurt. Toss all together except lettuce and spoon into lettuce leaves. Serve immediately.

DINNER | PIZZA | Vegetarian with Mixed Vegetables
Buy a pizza base. Dry-bake a range of prepared vegetables, to your taste. Try red onion, pumpkin, sweet potatoes, bell pepper and zucchini. Spread smoked eggplant dip on the base, add the baked vegetables and cover with fresh ricotta, arugula and avocado. Finish with a grind of black pepper and a drizzle of olive oil. Try an Italian variety wine with this dish or maybe an Australian-grown sangiovese.

DESSERT | Agar Agar
Dissolve agar in boiling water, carefully reading the instructions on the package. Add the same volume of fresh orange juice and pour over a bowl of any fresh berries (strawberries are best). Cool and set. Serve alone or with yoghurt.

Agar agar (KANTEN, CHINESE GEL). Asians are fond of moulded jellies (some from fruits and nut milks, but other made with sweetened beans and even corn), but many of these are jelled with a seaweed-derived gelatin called agar-agar (kanten in Japanese) rather than the gelatine derived from animal hooves and skins that is commonly used in Western cooking. For this reason, agar has been adopted by Western vegetarians and it is easily available in health food stores, in bar, flake and powder form. A further advantage over animal gelatine is that it will set at room temperature.

TIPS OF THE WEEK

Hunger pangs are sometimes in fact thirst signals. Have a cup of tea and the feeling will go away. If you are still challenged clean your teeth and have a glass of water.

Purchase the fresh shrimp on the weekend (or Monday) ready for tomorrow night's dinner.

Use red or green apples for the Waldorf salad or even both.

Depending on how your weight's going, drop a teaspoon of grated parmesan onto the cauliflower soup.

Shopping list

Bread rolls
(one per person)
Pumpernickel bread
Bread for wraps
Low fat yoghurt
Low fat ricotta cheese
Eggs
Mangos
Passionfruit
Pears or peaches
Berries
Oranges
Limes
Salad greens
Tomatoes
Lemongrass
Flat leaf parsley
Basil
Oregano
Coriander
Snowpeas
Bok choy
English spinach
Beetroot
Bell pepper
Red onion
Scallions
Ginger
Spring onions
Brown bean paste
Noodles
Napolitana sauce
Antipasto for pizza
Pizza base
Chicken fillets
Chicken for stir fry
Shrimps
Ham
Fish fillets
Blue swimmer crabs
Whole fish
Red wine
White wine
Chambourcin

Week 10: Expansive flavours

Reduce the amount of bread you are eating and increase the water, fruit and stir fry meals. Keep the portions small and supplement your meals with nuts and fruit if you need more. Don't be afraid to be hungry. It's okay sometimes to make yourself wait for the next meal. Green tea can be a favourite and will also reduce your appetite. From this week your pantry will have everything it needs for you to maintain a healthy, delicious eating plan.

	BREAKFAST	LUNCH	DINNER
MONDAY	FRUIT Fruit Salad & Yoghurt	BREAD Pumpernickel Sandwich	STIR FRY	DESSERT Shrimp & Vegetables Agar Agar (NEW)
TUESDAY	CEREAL Cooked Oatmeal	YOUR CHOICE	GRILL Grilled Chicken Fillets, Baked Beets & Rice Lime Juice Dressing ➡ to Wednesday Lunch
WEDNESDAY	GRAIN Corn Fritters with Wilted Spinach and Oven-Dried Tomatoes (NEW)	BREAD Chicken Fillets, Yoghurt & Salad Wrap	RICE Beet Risotto (NEW)
THURSDAY	FRUIT Poached Peaches or Pears	SALAD Large Garden Salad with Vinaigrette	GRILL Shrimp & Mango Salsa (NEW)
FRIDAY	CEREAL Cooked Oatmeal & Stewed Fruit	BREAD Ham & Salad Bread Roll	SOUP Carrot & Ginger (NEW)
SATURDAY	FRUIT Smoothie & Plain Toast	SEAFOOD Grilled Fish Fillets	PASTA Chili Blue Swimmer Crab & Egg Noodles (NEW)
SUNDAY	EGGS Poached with Tomatoes in Verjuice	BARBECUE Whole Fish (NEW)	PIZZA Gourmet with Antipasto (NEW)

Week 10

Monday

DINNER | STIR FRY | Shrimp & Green Vegetables

Heat the wok. Sizzle peanut oil. Cook lemongrass pieces, grated ginger and sliced garlic until lightly caramelised (1 min). Toss in Asian mixed green vegetables including snowpeas and bok choy. Cook shrimp separately then throw into the mix with a dash of stock or try rice wine here if you like. Stir together for a minute and then serve immediately. Season with light soy and oyster sauce.

DESSERT | Agar Agar

Remaining Agar from last night. Add passionfruit pulp or any stewed fruit plus a spoonful of low fat cottage cheese or ricotta cheese.

Wednesday

BREAKFAST | GRAIN | Corn Fritters with Wilted Spinach & Oven-Dried Tomatoes

Prepare the oven-dried tomatoes on the weekend or when you have a little time. Slice the tomatoes into halves and lie on baking paper in an oven tray. Chop fresh basil and oregano and sprinkle over with a generous grind of black pepper and a little sea salt. Place in the bottom of the oven on 210°F for 4-5 hours. Turn off and leave in the oven overnight if you can. If you make extra store them in an airtight jar having coated them with olive oil. Pour corn kernels and creamed corn into a bowl with diced bell pepper and onions and torn fresh coriander. Fold a small amount of self-raising flour into the mix to form a soft dough. Dollop into hot oiled skillet

Pantry list

Peanut oil
Truffle oil
Vanilla essence
Other wines to taste
Polenta
Cans of corn
(Whole kernels and creamed)
self-raising flour
Semolina
Wholemeal organic flour

and fry until brown each side. Quickly sauté the spinach and oven-dried tomatoes, then pile on top of the fritters. Moisten with lemon juice and olive oil.

DINNER | RICE | Beet Risotto

Cook risotto as before and add the cooked beets when you are adding the cheese just prior to serving. Stir it in to maximise the flavour and the colour effect.

Thursday

DINNER | GRILL | Shrimp & Mango Salsa

Remove the head and shell from the shrimps. Skewer ready for grilling. Drizzle olive oil and lemon juice over. Chop mangoes, red onion, red bell pepper and flat leaf parsley and combine in a bowl Squeeze lime juice over. Grill the shrimp, being careful not to overcook.

Chambourcin is a full-bodied red wine grown in Europe, Australia and the USA. It is usually grown near the coast, is a hardy grape variety and is a great accompaniment with strongly flavoured dishes such as chili crab, roast venison and most roasted or braised meat dishes. It can generally be purchased from your local liquor store. You will find that it is a pleasant wine style in a similar vein to other big hearty red wines.

Friday

DINNER | SOUP | Carrot & Ginger

Chop an onion and two garlic cloves. Sauté in hot olive oil with a pinch of mustard and a 1in piece of ginger peeled and grated. Chop 6 medium carrots and 2 sticks of celery and add to mix. Pour in 2 cups of homemade stock (any kind), bring to the boil, cover and simmer for 40 minutes. Blend and serve with a spoonful of yoghurt in each bowl.

Saturday

DINNER | PASTA | Chili Blue Swimmer Crab & Egg Noodles

Invite some friends and open a bottle of red wine to reward yourself for your progress. You'll need: 2 blue swimmers, 2 teaspoons each of ginger juice, spring onion juice and white wine, 2 tablespoons brown bean paste and 2 tablespoons brown sugar; ginger, chili and garlic to taste. Light soy sauce. 8 scallions, sliced. Noodles (cook and set aside as the crabs don't take long to cook). Note: Make the ginger and spring onion juice separately in a vegetable juicer - it's well worth the effort! Clean two large crabs. Cut and crack. Marinate for two hours in ginger juice, spring onion juice and wine. Stir fry in olive oil in a hot wok. Fry brown bean paste, ginger, dried chili, spring onion and garlic together. Add soy and sugar. Stir in and cook crab pieces for two minutes. Serve with egg noodles. Open your bottle of Chambourcin and enjoy the blending of flavours.

Sunday

LUNCH | BARBECUE | Whole Fish

Cook a quantity of rice. Wash cleaned and scaled fish. Place a knob of ginger and a bunch of fresh herbs inside the fish's cavity. Slice deep cuts across the flesh at its fattest and rub slithers of ginger and olive oil into the cuts. Wrap in baking paper and then in aluminum foil, drizzling a little olive oil over before sealing. Cook on top of the barbecue until meat is white and separates easily when pierced with a knife. Take out of the paper and place beside the rice on a serving dish. Squeeze fresh lemon juice over. Throw a small handful of fresh parsley over followed by a grind of fresh pepper. Heap with garden salad and a small amount of lime juice vinaigrette.

TIPS OF THE WEEK

Keep a few almonds and dried apricots handy to munch between meals.

Drink plenty of water.

Shopping list

Bread
Low fat milk
Low fat yoghurt
Feta cheese
Low fat cottage cheese
Parmesan cheese
Ricotta cheese
Large eggs
Pears or peaches
Apples
Passionfruit
Fruit for stewing
Salad greens
Tomatoes
Fresh herbs
Mint
Coriander
Cauliflower
Mushrooms
Green beans
Leeks
Avocado
Root vegetables for soup
Vegetables for juicing
Olives
Sun-dried tomatoes
Pepperoni
Artichokes
Other antipasto for pizza
Chicken stock
Red lentils
Moroccan spice
Napolitana sauce
Prunes
Ground beef
Chicken
Fresh shrimps
Whole fish
Veal for braise
Red wine
Sweet wine or fortified port

Week 11: Going gourmet

Pizza on polenta base, frittata, whole fish, veal braise, nasi goreng and more meals lead you to become a more interesting cook. Expand your cooking now with favourite ingredients (and keep the Flavour Diet going, not just for another week but until you reach your goal of being a healthier and stronger person). Enjoy new flavours and textures for the rest of your life and share your newfound experiences and lifestyle with others.

	BREAKFAST	LUNCH	DINNER
MONDAY	EGGS Omelet & Sautéed Fresh Mushrooms	YOUR CHOICE	PASTA Spaghetti Bolognaise with Salad
TUESDAY	FRUIT Fruit, Fruit, Fruit	SALAD Garden Salad & Cheese	PIZZA Gourmet Antipasto on Polenta Base *NEW*
WEDNESDAY	FRUIT Poached Peaches or Pears with Cottage Cheese	FRUIT Fruit Juice	EGGS Potato Frittata & Salad *NEW*
THURSDAY	CEREAL Cooked Oatmeal & Stewed Fruit Lemon or Green Tea	BREAD | FRUIT Crunchy Bread Roll, Fresh Fruit, Yoghurt & Green Tea	RICE Nasi Goreng *NEW*
FRIDAY	BREAD French Toast *NEW*	FRUIT Fruit & Almonds	YOUR CHOICE
SATURDAY	GRAIN Corn Fritters with Ricotta Cheese	BARBECUE Whole Fish	SOUP | PASTA Cauliflower with Truffle Oil Egg Noodles with Mushrooms & Green Beans *NEW*
SUNDAY	YOUR CHOICE Make it light	SOUP Moroccan Red Lentil Soup *NEW*	BRAISE | DESSERT Veal Zurich Fruit in Wine *NEW* ⇨ to Monday Dinner

Week 11

Tuesday

DINNER | PIZZA | Gourmet Antipasto on Polenta Base
Pre-heat the oven to 350°F/180°C. To make the base, bring homemade stock to the boil in a large saucepan. Turn down the heat and slowly add the instant polenta, whisking constantly to avoid lumps. Add grated parmesan and a little knob of butter. When the polenta is thick and comes away from the sides (about 10 minutes) it is ready. Sparsely oil the bottom of a pizza pan, pour over the polenta and bake for 30 minutes or until slightly crisp. Spread Napolitana sauce, feta cheese, olives, sun-dried tomatoes, pepperoni, artichokes and any other favourite antipasto pieces over the base and bake for a further 10 minutes at 320°F/180°C. Serve with a glass of red wine.

Wednesday

DINNER | EGGS | Potato Frittata & Salad
Prepare as for omelet, adding parmesan for a richer taste. Make a generous skillet full of thinly sliced cooked potato and brown onions. Pour the egg mix over the potato and onions in the skillet and cook on the stovetop. When half cooked through, brown under the griller. Serve with green salad. Keep your frittata portion small and the salad portion large!

Thursday

DINNER | RICE | Nasi Goreng
Stir fry chicken strips and shrimp separately and set aside. Boil brown rice until soft and nutty. Add a pinch of turmeric powder, a small pinch of chili powder, chicken, shrimps, season with sweet soy and finish with heaps of fresh coriander.

Friday

BREAKFAST | BREAD | French Toast
Beat an egg with 1 tablespoon of milk and a small splash of vanilla essence. Heat a skillet on the stovetop. Toss in a small knob of butter. Dip one slice of bread into the egg mixture till coated. Fry both sides of the bread. Serve with slices of fresh fruit in season. Espresso coffee is great here.

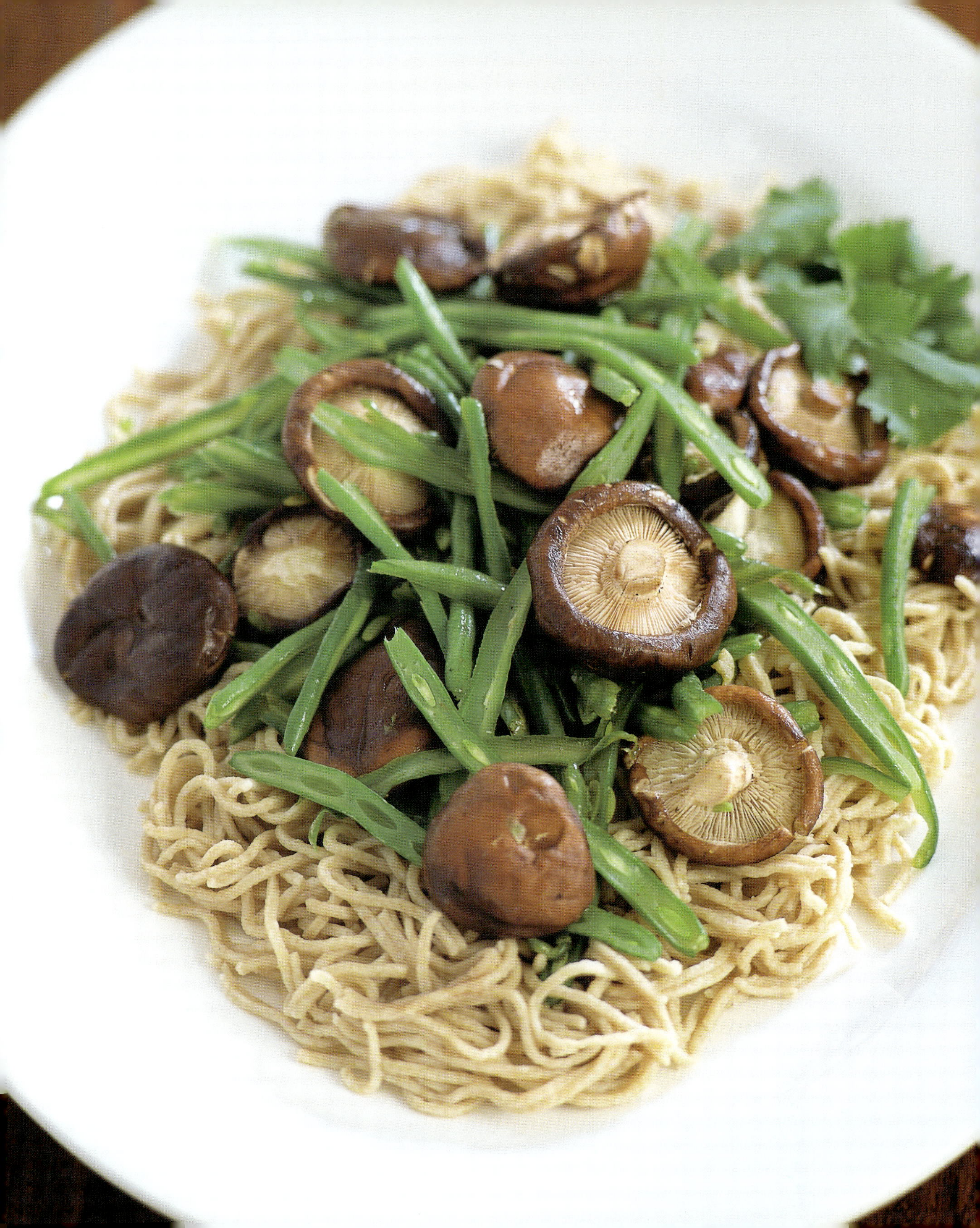

Week 11

Saturday

DINNER | SOUP/PASTA | Cauliflower & White Truffle Oil Soup and Egg Noodles with Mushrooms & Green Beans

Soup as for Saturday week 9.

For the noodles: 90g/3oz semolina, 440g/14oz wholewheat organic flour, 6 large eggs, 3 teaspoons of salt. Sautéed mushrooms and steamed green beans to serve. Sift semolina and flour, break eggs into the centre and add salt. Incorporate eggs into the flour with your hands, drawing flour mixture into the egg until a coarse paste is formed. If the mixture is too sticky, add more flour. Knead dough with your palms on a lightly floured surface. Work the dough for 10-15 minutes until smooth and elastic. Cover in plastic wrap and rest for an hour. Gently roll out into a rectangle sheet about $1/10$th of an inch thick. Slice or use a pasta machine to form noodles. Cook as soon as possible or dry over a clean coat hanger for 10 minutes. Boil noodles for 5-8 minutes in water with sea salt and a dash of oil added. Strain and top with sautéed mushrooms and green beans.

TIP OF THE WEEK

Keep the dessert portions low and treat these as rewards at the end of an effective weight loss week.

Sunday

LUNCH | SOUP | Moroccan Red Lentil Soup

Stir a teaspoon of Moroccan spice in olive oil until aromatic. Add chicken stock, a can of crushed tomatoes and grated ginger and peeled and diced root vegetables. Simmer for half an hour with the red lentils and finish with coriander and heaps of fresh mint.

DINNER | BRAISE | Veal Zurich

Sauté diced brown onion, a teaspoon of sugar, garlic, bay leaves and sliced mushrooms. Cut veal into strips and coat with plain flour. Add meat to sautéed vegetables and lightly cook for 2 minutes or until brown. Add chicken stock and a glass of red wine and simmer for half an hour. Place in the oven to develop the flavours further until cooked well through. Slow cooking on a lower heat here will embellish the flavours. Finish on the stovetop. Shake all particles loose and add a good splash of the best wine you have a few minutes before serving. Accompany with basmati rice or noodles.

DESSERT | Prunes, Peaches or Pears in Wine

Gently stew the fruit in sweet wine. Place in a sealable container. Sweet wine with the peaches and pears and a fortified port with the prunes make a great SMALL dessert after an evening meal.

Shopping list

Bread
Low fat milk
Low fat yoghurt
Low fat cottage cheese
Parmesan cheese
Eggs
Fruit (include some for smoothies)
Oranges
Salad greens
Tomatoes
Pumpkin
Stir fry vegetables
Braise vegetables (include turnips)
Celery
Cabbage
Fresh herbs
Basil for pesto
Can of white beans
Can of kidney beans
Can of borlotti beans
Olives
Sun-dried tomatoes
Antipasto for pizza
Star anise
Vanilla beans
Fish fillets
Cooked chicken
Chicken bones for stock
Chicken pieces for soup
Fresh duck pieces
Pinot Noir

Week 12: Last formal week of the Flavour Diet

You are coming to the end of the 12 week Rescue Me Flavour Diet, but it's not over. Please keep cooking your food for flavour and for health. Portion control is the strongest message we can leave you with. Enjoy the food and most of all where possible share your table with others as the shared table is an essential ingredient when planning your meal.

	BREAKFAST	LUNCH	DINNER
MONDAY	YOUR CHOICE	BREAD Chicken & Salad Sandwich	PIE Shepherd's Pie *NEW*
TUESDAY	CEREAL Cooked Oatmeal & Honey	CHEESE Cottage Cheese, Almonds & a sprinkle of Raisins	FISH Grilled Fish Fillets & Salad
WEDNESDAY	FRUIT Lemon or Green Tea	SOUP Pumpkin Soup with Nutmeg	YOUR CHOICE
THURSDAY	FRUIT Smoothie	SOUP Minestrone	PIZZA On Polenta Base
FRIDAY	FRUIT Fresh Fruit Salad Any Tea	PIZZA with Salad	STIR FRY Stir Fry, Stir Fry
SATURDAY	GRAIN Corn Fritters	PASTA Pesto Pasta & Pinenuts *NEW*	BRAISE Vegetables Stewed Fruit
SUNDAY	EGGS Poached in Verjuice	SOUP Chicken Soup	ROAST Double Cooked Duck *NEW* ➡ Next Week

Monday

DINNER | PIE | Shepherd's Pie

Place the Veal Zurich leftovers into a pie dish. Boil enough potatoes (leave skins on) to mash and top the contents of the pie dish. Sprinkle a little cheese on top and bake in the oven at 350°F/180°C for 20 minutes or until brown. Serve with a crisp green salad and a good grind of black pepper. Drizzle a little vinaigrette dressing over. Keep the portion small with the emphasis on the salad.

Saturday

LUNCH | PASTA | Pesto Pasta & Pinenuts

Sprinkle a handful of pinenuts into a gently oiled fry pan. Stir over a moderate heat until brown. Take one handful of dry pasta per person. Boil the pasta. Mix in a spoonful of basil pesto and sprinkle pinenuts over. Add a small amount of grated parmesan. To make the pesto: blend one cup of basil leaves, ½ cup of virgin olive oil, 1oz/30g pinenuts, 2 cloves crushed garlic, pinch of sea salt and 2oz/60g of freshly grated parmesan cheese. Blend everything except the cheese, which you stir into the bright green pesto after it's blended. Purchase fresh pasta where possible, as this will give the best results. If you are truly keen to develop your talents in the kitchen, buy or borrow a pasta maker. It will come with ample instructions on how make your own – and it's certainly worth the effort.

Continue to experiment with taste and flavour: expand your cooking skills at every opportunity and this will keep your healthy eating and exercise habits going. If you have learnt to expand your flavour horizons and have fun with food you will practise smaller portions and keep the new skills as part of your new lifestyle. Keep going now with your own plans including your exercise program

TIPS OF THE WEEK

Get into the habit of drinking lemon or green tea with your breakfasts.

Make fresh vegetable juices several days a week and keep yourself well hydrated during the day with water and teas, especially after exercising.

Make the soup on Sunday with homemade stock. See Wednesday Week 5.

Sunday

DINNER | ROAST | Double Cooked Duck

Deglaze a large saucepan with a splash of pinot noir. Add 1 tablespoon virgin olive oil and brown the duck pieces. Add 2 cloves of garlic, a knob of fresh ginger and enough chicken stock to cover $1/3$ of the pieces. Simmer, turning frequently, until tender. Leave in the juice overnight. Remove from liquid and place in deep baking dish. Add a splash of olive oil, pieces of peeled orange, juice from the oranges, star anise and vanilla beans. Bake at 380°/200°CF until crispy, turning frequently. Serve with fresh orange pieces, green olives and pour cooking juice over. Enjoy with boiled wild rice and a glass of pinot noir.

Don't forget to reserve a piece of duck to merge with a tasty risotto for next week.

A risotto secret

Traditionally risotto is cooked while standing with it and stirring the stock into it every minute of the process. A wonderful discovery is oven-baked risotto. Place the risotto rice in a baking dish. Cover three times its height with stock. Sprinkle over a generous handful of sliced mushrooms or half cooked pumpkin cubes and spread grated cheese over the top. Season with cracked pepper and salt. Cover with double layers of foil and place in the oven at 350°F/180 °C for 30 minutes. It will be cooked and ready to serve and how easy was that!

Chapter 6
Winemakers, chefs and heavenly flavours

Chapter 6: Winemakers, chefs and heavenly flavours

You have read the Flavour Diet so now you will be further introduced to the pleasures of understanding flavours and tastes and to the excitement of giving your palate (as well as your body) a workout. When you replace a portion of your meal with increased flavour you will raise the bar in enjoyment and assist your waistline at the same time. This chapter looks at food, wine, more food, more wine and how to put it all together.

An important aim of the exercise and food plans is to give you the foundation you need to change your life for the long run. You will have realised by now that you can alter and improve many aspects of your lifestyle. Exercising, cooking and eating-smart can be a great deal of fun and at the same time give you the satisfaction of physical improvement. It's time now to reject the notion that other people can decide what you eat. It's time to celebrate the diversity and seasonality of foods. And it's time to taste and appreciate the flavour of food and drink - smell it, chew it, enjoy it and make it an experience every day.

Flavour combines the messages of smell and taste. To enjoy a flavour to its fullest, however, all the senses need to interact with each other. Flavour is not a sense and should be clearly distinguished from taste. There are five primary tastes: sweet, sour, salt, bitter and umami (food with a rich, powerful flavour). Your newfound interest in freshness, flavours and discovering new ingredients provides you with many interesting opportunities to explore taste and smell, and these will help you along the road to rescue. In combination with the smaller servings associated with portion control, as outlined in the the Rescue Me food plan, you'll be eating better and still losing weight.

The western diet has changed substantially as the influence of multiculturalism takes effect, bringing new produce and ways of cooking to our kitchens. Information available via the internet and television means we are all able to experiment with different ethnic culinary styles. There is a wonderful range of fresh herbs and spices available at produce markets and in most supermarkets. The growth in the international export and import of fresh foods means we are exposed to a potential flavour revolution.

You will now understand more about the wonders of flavour. The stories will unfold and you will appreciate the intricacies and importance of flavour as you never have before.

Dr Max Lake, an internationally recognised Australian food and wine expert and prolific author in the area of taste and flavour for food and wine, has written Lake's Laws of Flavour to give a greater understanding of the magic of flavour. Immutable laws of flavour apply to humans, at least as constant as Isaac Newton's Laws of Motion. Lake's Laws? You be the judge.

Lake's First Law of Flavour
**Sight dominates smell.
The eye has the first bite.**

Life can be beautiful and you can make it so. Presentation matters. The attention you pay to serving a well-structured meal in the correct bowl or on the right plate will make all the difference to how meals are received by others. Burnt or pale, uninteresting food, poorly presented, will not be received well - and the opposite to that, of course, is that well-presented food will be well received and eaten with enthusiasm. A beautiful plate (wiped clean of splatters), appropriate linen and the right glass used at the shared table can have the desired effect even if the meal is good but not great.

A small hi-rise pub in Shiajuku Tokyo sells a dish of five kinds of seaweed. Each is a different colour and they all look extremely mouthwatering and appetising. After you eat it you realise that each has the same taste - the eye certainly has the first bite! You can also apply this law when preparing meals for children who are not interested in food - a ninja turtle decoration on a plate can make the difference between the food being eaten or not.

Lake's Second Law of Flavour
Taste is the frame of a flavour, smell is its cladding.

Think of the structure of a building and relate that to the structure of the flavour. The senses of taste and smell interact. Sweet taste increases perception of fragrance. Umami enhances flavour. Sourness lifts the middle flavour and low acidity flattens it. It's not enough for food to look wonderful - the smell must be impressive too!

When a tasty meal is put before us, our immediate response is to bend forward and smell it. The aroma of the food completes our acceptance of the meal. For people of all ages and races, the smell of food is what comes before eating it. Those that understand and enjoy wine will have a great big sniff as part of identifying the wine and establishing their expectation of the taste.

Mike Dobrovic of the Mulderbosh Winery in South Africa comments: "Lake's Second Law of Flavour reminds me of an unforgettable meal that I had just after I was married. I spent part of my youth in Kimberly - between Africa's Karoo semi desert and the Kalahari

Desert. The Karoo plants started to diversify about 260 million years ago. The Kalahari is the oldest desert in the world, so also has wonderful diversity. Many of the herbaceous shrubs have wonderful perfumes and the buck and sheep that eat these plants have a particular flavour to their meat.

"Needless to say, I was brought up eating the local lamb. Years after when I was married and living in Stellenbosch in South Africa, some friends came down from Kimberly with a gift of half a lamb for us. My wife roasted the leg with a little chardonnay, an onion or two and a few carrots and potatoes. She also added some salt. When I walked into the house, the aroma of the roasting lamb brought back a flood of memories. Smells that I had forgotten had returned. I was overcome with emotions, evoked simply by that particular dish of lamb. Of course the taste was exquisite, in no small part due to the memories brought back by the extraordinary smell."

Lake's Third Law of Flavour

Mood subdues flavour and fragrance. Good manners spoil good food. Memory, emotion and ambience influence appreciation.

Sharing food and drink causes a rise in happy hormones. Take time out with your partner to go to a special place (maybe your favourite hideaway in the woods or at the beach) to eat that special meal. Use the time to get to know each other better, to be intimate - to simply enjoy everything around you.

Preparing food with your hands and sometimes eating it with your hands is seen by some as bad manners. However, it can enhance your appreciation of the meal. Enjoy rubbing the oil and the rosemary into the lamb. Pick up the chop, the prawn or the vegetable and enjoy the feel of the food. Understand the sensuality of food and deepen your knowledge of texture and flavour. Share meals with others where and when you can. Make every meal a feast even if it's small and quick.

When eating at home avoid doing so in front of the television or computer - engage in conversation around the table and communicate through the wonderful medium of food. Try saying "…and how was your day?" You may be surprised by the answer!

Lake's Fourth Law of Flavour

Less is more. The paradox of pleasure. Flavour and fragrance are best enjoyed at threshold.

This law emphasises the beauty of simplicity. Be restrained with spices as over-use can ruin a meal. Adding too many bay leaves to a rich meat dish can cruel the flavour. A meal's flavour and fragrance are at their best when the meal is first before you. Dressing the meal with appropriate garnishes will immediately increase the pleasure of those eating it. A little lemon, ginger, pepper or vinaigrette adds not only flavour, but also to increased enjoyment of the meal from the outset. An aroma that's too strong can be a turn-off, especially for children. If you are introducing someone to a new flavour such as rosemary, keep the effect small in the first place and gradually build up the flavour in subsequent meals.

Lake's Fifth Law of Flavour
Mixtures.
More than one aroma in a sniff.

An average person can identify three separate aromas in a mix - more than that is a waste. Experts can identify up to five.

Flavour experts are few and far between, however, so when planning a meal, spend a minute considering the end flavour you are trying to achieve. Don't include more than three main flavours in the dish.

A rather special application of this law with spectacular results is apple and rhubarb crumble with a matching yet contrasting sour cream topping. Stew the fruit (1) and bake with a flour or dry oats (2) and butter (3) crumble. Now mix a little sour cream (1) with a small helping of castor sugar (2). Now for the twist - add in a good touch of mustard powder (3). The resulting cream topping is interesting and rich and only a very small dollop is required to create a balance with the fruit crumble.

Individual tastes will show up some rather unique flavour mixes: as a youthful romantic it's not impossible to be passionate about ice cream (1) with chocolate topping (2) eaten in the same instant as hot potato chips sprinkled with salt (3). Each to his or her own!

Lake's Sixth Law of Flavour
The flavour and fragrance of living things derive from their source. What we eat tastes of what it eats (or subsists on).

Have you ever considered that there are different flavours in wild versus farmed birds and animals? Wild crocodile versus farmed croc. Wild boar versus farmed pigs. Free range chickens versus caged chickens. Wild duck versus farmed duck. Wild rabbit versus farmed rabbit. Wild trout versus farmed trout and so on…

Executive Chef Hamish Unahi draws on his New Zealand training and high-level experience both in Papua New Guinea and Australia when he talks of using wild versus farmed produce in his kitchen.

"I was sitting in my office in a five star hotel in Port Moresby when one of my staff alerted me to a local fisherman at the back door with some fresh produce. I like to purchase from the locals when I can so I said he should be asked in to show me what he had. A small fisherman came in dragging a 10-foot crocodile. Of course it ended up on the menu, mainly because I love the fresh gamey flavours of wild animals. Those local crocs tasted of goat, birds and fish. Their firm muscular flesh is the result of the stress they suffer in the competitive wild. They fight, run fast and eat the local prey, and their flesh tastes of what they eat!"

It's a known fact that farmed crocodile has soft flesh and tastes of chicken with hints of fish flavours, due to a staple diet of raw chicken and fish. Wild boars spend a great deal of time fighting for food and they also develop firm flesh as a result. Their end flavour is that of rabbit and any other local prey they happen upon. Similarly, venison has a gamey, rich taste, which with careful preparation and cooking will result in umami flavours. Farmed animals don't have the gamey flavours of their wild brothers and sisters.

A corn-fed chicken is a good example of

the direct effects of feed on the resulting meat, with the yellow colour and corn flavour very evident when it's cooked. Free-range chickens are usually bigger than their caged cousins. They eat grass, bugs and worms and as a result develop a tasty marbled fat in their flesh.

Wild ducks fly great distances and their metabolism is more aggressive than their caged counterparts. Their flesh is leaner and firmer than the farmed birds. Similarly, wild trout is a lower fat-content fish as it expends a great deal of energy racing upstream and fighting for survival, while the farmed variety has a lazy life swimming in ponds, with time to develop fat.

In the same way, the taste and flavour of wine is derived from the soil and climate of the locality. This is generally referred to as the 'terroir' of the region.

Culinary thrills: what excites the experts?

HAMISH UNAHI'S favourite meal is a sugar banana. "I kept one or two hands of bananas hanging in my office in Port Moresby so that I always had a quick meal on hand and bananas are still my choice."

DR MAX LAKE says that his 'escape velocity' is achieved with a chunk broken from the middle of a wedge of a sweet old cheese like parmesan, fresh crusty wood-fired or stone-baked white bread made from hard wheat and a firm red wine, with a sweet crunchy pear to finish.

JAMES HEALEY, winemaker at Dog Point Vineyards in New Zealand, reports that he fell from his chair in delight having experienced a sensitively prepared whitebait omelet (that is, three times the weight of bait to egg) finished under the grill, paired with chablis. "The delicacy of flavour of the whitebait matched with the dry minerality of the wine is incredible."

GEORGE TSIROS of the Hunter Valley in Australia nominates his favourite meal match as Sydney rock oysters gently marinated in French champagne and lime juice. The acid in the champagne and the lime juice destroys the bacteria. Garnish the oysters with lump fish roe or caviar and a slim strip of lox. This elegant meal takes George to his idea of taste heaven.

For Hunter Valley executive chef **DARREN HO**, a personal flavour peak is reached with his wife Sandy when they share yum cha on a Sunday morning. If they are eating before noon they drink Chinese tea - after noon it's Chinese beer, a perfect match to the Chinese brunch.

Ho specialises in matching food with wine. One of his famous matches is the rather tricky combination of barbecue duck and sweet pickled lemons, paired with a young Australian pinot noir from Victoria. In a controversial match for his sea scallops stuffed with water chestnuts Ho chooses a sweet botrytis semillon. The late-picked wine's sweet apricot flavour pairs brilliantly with the scallops, and its smooth stickiness complements the chestnut flavour of the stuffing to a standard of excellence. The careful addition of a tiny touch of tomato olive paste brings the taste and the texture into balance.

CAJ AND GENNY AMADIO formerly of Chain of Ponds winery in the Adelaide Hills explore their Italian heritage through their everyday cooking and have a special love for seafood. When on Kangaroo Island they like to track down some local freshwater shrimp to gently barbecue and serve with fresh salads. The delicate flavour of the shrimp is best matched with an equally delicate riesling.

Eat, drink and maximise flavour

Wine consumed in moderation is a wonderful way to add flavour to your meal. A glass of red wine each day is said to have very positive effects on the health of your heart while at the same time adding flavour to many foods. Deglazing a pan with the wine to be consumed with the meal is an excellent flavour-bridge from the cooked food to the wine. Deglazing the barbecue with wine makes a similar bridge.

Use good wine glasses and, if you can, purchase some crystal glasses in order to make every wine occasion a special event. Even at a casual picnic or an outdoor barbecue, use wine glasses and not plastic as glasses are part of the wine-drinking ritual.

When considering flavours and taste, wine can be a very special part of your meal. If you are serving small portions at mealtime and preparing meals with extra flavour in an effort to maximise your rescue plan, complete your new experience by having fun matching wine and food flavours.

Ask the person behind the wine store counter, the sommelier in the restaurant or even the winemaker (quite often their web address is on the bottle) for some wine and food-matching suggestions. You'll be surprised how much difference it can make to get the combination right. The wine books in your local library or bookstore can also introduce you to new ideas.

California's Napa Valley is a favourite haunt of many tourists from around the world. The boutique wine cellars and restaurants are places of secret flavours and food-matching recipes. The Valley specialises in chardonnay, semillon, sauvignon blanc, cabernet and shiraz varieties which match well with seasonal gourmet foods. Winemakers love to tell you which food is best matched to their wine and there are some very innovative matching secrets that come from behind the cellar doors. Cabernet with chocolate mud cake and merlot matched to fish casserole cooked in a tomato base are two of the more controversial suggestions.

Taste testing wine

Taste testing wine is not necessarily elegant. To enjoy the full experience, take a good mouthful and draw air into the mouth through the wine. This makes a gurgling sound, but it's essential in order to magnify the wine's volatile characteristics in the back of the throat. The aromas are then picked up by a patch of olfactory epithelium at the back of the nose where they are automatically analysed and transmitted to the brain as a chemical flavour.

'Slurping' the wine in your mouth like this may raise a few laughs from friends, so maybe practise it alone as it's a valuable skill to have if you are interested in assessing wines when planning your cellar or simply shopping for the next dinner.

First impressions on taking the wine into the mouth may be referred to as the fore palate, followed by the mid and end palate, leading up to the finish. The finish describes the sensations derived from swallowing the wine. If the taste lingers, the wine is said to have good finish or good length. The more length a wine has, the more time you have to enjoy it, and it's probably true to say that these wines are generally of better quality.

When you smell chocolate (or cinnamon, licorice, vanilla and so on) in your wine it's not because someone dropped a chocolate chip in your glass. It's because a certain group of chemicals in the wine is identical to that in a chocolate chip!

Flavours you may detect in wine include:

Spices and herbs: cinnamon, cloves, black pepper and licorice

Fruits: apple, apricot, banana, black currant, cherry, citrus, lychee, mango, melon, peach, pear, plum and raisin

Flowers: rose and violet

Berries: blackberry, raspberry and strawberry

Vegetables: asparagus and capsicum

Nuts: general nuttiness, hazelnut and almonds

Plants: grass, oak, tea, tobacco and wood

Others: Leather, wet leather, forest floor, wet cardboard and wet dog's hair.

Match delicate wines with delicate foods and heavy wines with robust tucker.

What wines with which foods – some rules of thumb

Acidic wines work well with salty dishes. For example, oysters are briny, with an oily mouth-coating texture that can smother most wines. However, a sparkling wine from California, a Spanish cava or French champagne can both refresh and cleanse your palate when eating seafood.

Hot spices in Asian, Thai, curry and chili pepper dishes can numb the palate. Many of these foods also have high acidity from citrus ingredients such as lime juice as well as sweetness. Therefore, you need a wine with an acidic backbone as well as a touch of sweetness, such as an off-dry California sparkling wine with lots of fruit.

Off-dry acidic wines go well with many dishes; however, two of the most difficult wines to pair with food are also the two of the most popular: chardonnay and cabernet sauvignon. Some chardonnays can be oaky, buttery, flavourful wines that overwhelm many dishes. But you can still enjoy chardonnay with your meal. Pair it with butter and cream sauces to marry similar textures and flavours.

Cabernet sauvignons can have bitter dark fruit flavours with mouth-drying tannins, therefore they find their happiest match in foods with juicy proteins such as a rare steak. The protein softens the tannin, making the wine taste smooth and fruity. Steaks cooked with crushed black peppercorns sensitise your taste buds, making the wine taste even more fruity and robust. However, the preparation of the dish is also a factor. A well-done steak, for example, may taste too dry with a tannic cabernet.

Proteins are also at work with the marriage of wine and cheese, the cocktail classic. Red wines tend to go better with blue cheese as they can accommodate more tannins. However, white wines suit soft cheeses such as brie and camembert as the creamier textures require more acidity for balance.

Game birds such as quail, pheasant, turkey, duck, squab and guinea hen have earthy flavours that are more robust than chicken. Wild game often goes better with racy red wines that have a gamey quality to them, the classic being Burgundian pinot noir. The flavours of pinot noir - plum, cherry,

Did you know that tannins are a family of natural organic compounds found in grape skins, seeds and stems? As well, during the wine's aging process oak barrels infuse tannin into the juice. They are an excellent antioxidant and preservative; they also help to give the wine structure and texture. Tannins provide an important flavour dimension in wine. If you bite into a grape seed, the woody taste is tannin.

mushrooms, earth and even barnyard (that's a positive adjective) - accentuate the same gamey flavours in the food. Other wine options for game birds include Spanish rioja, Oregon pinot noir and lighter-style Rhône Valley wines such as Côte-Rôtie.

One of the most challenging flavours to balance is sweetness. Dishes with a touch of sweetness such as glazed pork do well with off-dry wines such as riesling and chenin blanc. However, rich desserts such as chocolate and crème brulée demand a wine that is sweeter than the dessert, or the wine will taste thin, even bitter. Sweet wines such as sauternes, Canadian ice-wine, late harvest wines and port will work not only for their sweetness but also for their unctuous texture.

To make a statement, a wine doesn't have be above 13.5% alcohol.

Don't overpower the flavour of the food with ill-matched wines. Save your big gutsy reds for big umami flavours, big complicated foods and even big chocolate mud cakes!

Cooking with wine
- an experience easily missed yet easily learnt

Wine is often used in cooking to impart flavour to a meal. The flavour of wine is absorbed into the ingredients during the cooking process, and the alcohol evaporates, leaving a soft, palatable wine flavour imbued in the dish.

Don't be fooled into thinking that the wine you cook with can be of inferior quality. Use good wine as it adds quality flavours to good food. Generally use the same wine in the cooking as you will be serving with the meal as the flavours will then be in harmony (unless it's a Penfold's Grange then use a lesser quality). Add a little of the (best) wine to the dish immediately prior to serving as this gives a special lift to the flavour. A splash of red wine into the baking dish, stirred and reduced, will deliver a tasty sauce or garnish for the meal. Try splashing a little port into the baking dish after cooking a beef or lamb roast and you will be rewarded handsomely.

This wine goes with … Some quick tips

CHAMPAGNE goes well with anything, with anyone and at any time. It has been said that simply for the purpose of celebrating the afternoon, a bottle of chilled champagne in a champagne flute is warranted. If you are serving this wine before dinner, keep a little to have at the end of the meal with a sweet dish.

SEMILLON is best served with crabmeat, prawns and mussels; monkfish or any of the meatier types of fish, simply grilled; any fish or seafood (especially lobster) served in buttery, nutty, hollandaise- or thermidor-type sauces; potato-topped fish pie; lox and other smoked fish; duck à l'orange; omelets filled with mushrooms and/or cheese; avocado; vegetable terrines; Chinese sweet corn soup; some of the creamier Indian dishes such as korma; or the vindaloo dishes. Also serve it with poultry such as turkey or a Cornish hen. Semillon should happily stand up to both red and white meat roasts as the occasion demands, especially when served with creamy sauces.

RIESLING is a very versatile wine and is wonderful with oysters as it does not overpower the delicate taste. A gastronomically-inclined Frenchman, Charles Richet, is said to have discovered that the lemon juice added to raw oysters before eating them destroys 92 per cent of the bacteria present within 15 minutes. A good reason to wait before you eat! Serve also with shellfish with fruity or exotically flavoured dressings; with avocado salad; cold duck breast; stir-fried or poached dishes such as poached sole; sun-dried tomatoes; and roast vegetables.

UNOAKED CHARDONNAY needs its delicate profile matched with equally delicate food such as simple shellfish or freshwater fish dishes; summer salads with soft (not acidic!) dressings; asparagus and artichokes; Thailand's bean sprouts and noodles; and bowls of pasta dribbled with pesto, the best quality virgin olive oil, or garlic butter. It will also show an affinity for cheese-and-egg dishes, as long as the food is not too creamy or buttery.

SAUVIGNON BLANC is a very useful wine to serve whenever sharp seasonings and a certain amount of acidity in the food (for example goat's cheese) demand a sharply textured wine. Because of its good acidity, it will be the perfect match for salads dressed in vinaigrette. Tomatoes will not frighten it either. On the contrary, it will instantly fall in love with tomatoes in every form! It should also be brilliant with asparagus, simply steamed and served with a touch of lemon-butter or a green-pepper sauce; with asparagus quiche; oysters on the half-shell; seafood salads; and Thai food.

VERDELHO works well with Middle Eastern foods such as megadarra, a rice and lentil dish.

ROSÉ marries with the rough texture of shark or tuna and is good with many fish dishes, especially with salmon and pink-fleshed trout; with cooked lobster dishes; and seafood soup or stew. Its typical pinotage character means it works very well with baked ham, Peking duck, rabbit casserole, ratatouille, paella, antipasti, Japanese teriyaki, dim sum, and hot Thai noodle dishes.

PINOT NOIR has a wonderful complexity that makes it a natural match with duck cooked in any manner at all: roast, barbecue, Asian-style or merged into a risotto or cold salad. Side dishes of ribbon noodles, fennel, celery, red cabbage, Brussels sprouts, mushrooms and both white and black truffles are also simply perfect with a pinot noir. For a very special occasion, chill the wine well and serve with a bowl of ripe strawberries or raspberries (without cream and sugar).

SWEET WINES are well matched to lox (yes), a range of cheeses, meringue desserts such as pavlova, and lemon tarts.

SPARKLING REDS (shiraz, cabernet or merlot), nicely chilled, go well with a rich curry or roast turkey at Thanksgiving dinner.

ITALIAN VARIETIES (such as sangiovese, dolcetto, nebbiolo, and barbera) are really worth tracking down and matching up with your favourite Italian foods. These Italian reds are best with tomato-based dishes. Also seek out a bottle of the tempranillo variety and you can enjoy it pre-dinner with a pecorino or parmesan cheese.

Try **PINOT GRIS** (pinot grigio) with linguine and prosciutto for a light trip into the fantastic.

BORDEAUX BLEND such as cabernet merlot complements rabbit casserole braised with vegetables (use it in the cooking too).

SHIRAZ is a full-bodied style of wine with enough stamina to happily partner even the most substantial food. It works with umami flavours and tastes such as barbecue meat and stands up to all those intensely-flavoured dishes which tend to overpower most other soft-centered red wines: roast venison, beef and lamb served with reduction, berry and chocolate-chili sauces, rich casseroles such as oxtail or beef bourguignon, and baked dishes incorporating beef, lamb, pork, various types of sausages, beans and lentils. It also takes to spicy seasonings like a duck to water. Shiraz does not go with North Indian foods because of the curry flavours.

CABERNET'S classic match would be roast lamb, but it should also perform very well when paired with other plainly-served red meats like a chateaubriand. Also serve it with meaty casseroles, steaks, uncluttered poultry or game-bird dishes (especially roast chicken, turkey, duck and quail), and burgers made with best-quality minced beef. Side dishes of potatoes, broccoli, mushrooms and carrots work well with cabernet, but strong spices, fish or shellfish, sweetish sauces or cream do not. Cabernet also matches well with hard cheese and coffee after dinner.

Mulled Port

A marriage made in heaven on a cold night with a few warm friends.

Makes six (6oz) glasses.

2 oranges
12 whole cloves
1/2 teaspoon ground mace
1/2 teaspoon grated nutmeg
1/2 teaspoon ground allspice
1 cinnamon stick
1/4 cup sugar
1 cup water
750 ml bottle quality port

Place the sliced peel of one orange in a large non-reactive saucepan. Add cloves, mace, nutmeg, allspice, cinnamon stick, sugar and the water. Set over a medium-high heat and stir frequently to dissolve the sugar. Allow the liquid to reach the boil and turn down to medium heat. Simmer for 10 minutes. Strain the mixture and return to the pan. Add port and heat, but do not boil. Serve in Irish coffee glasses with a thin slice of orange in each.

Enjoy!

Chapter 7
Childhood obesity and the big fat truth

Chapter 7: Childhood obesity and the big fat truth

Go back to the mirror. This time you see the reflection of your naked children looking back at you. But do you have the courage to see them as they really are? Do you realise that they are overweight, unfit and potential candidates for type 2 diabetes and other diseases because of the environment you have created for them? Do you blame the school, television, video games or your local government for closing the neighbourhood park? Instead, reflect on the food and exercise behaviours you put in place for your children during their infancy and early childhood, let alone their teenage years and beyond. How much are your children imitating you?

Childhood obesity is a major health concern worldwide. Not only is it a growing epidemic, but the rate at which it's growing is accelerating. In the US, the number of overweight children aged six to 11 has tripled over the past 30 years. In Britain, 25 per cent of children suffer from obesity, as do 20-25 per cent of Australian children. China is super-sizing its children as fast as its economy, prompting fears of an American-style obesity crisis in Asia.

With such statistics comes the frightening fact that large numbers of children are presenting to hospitals with metabolic syndrome and type 2 diabetes, once a disease of the elderly.

Preventing obesity is an essential part of raising healthy, fit kids. The more overweight a child is, the greater the risk of metabolic syndrome leading to type 2 diabetes and of mental health and social issues.

Metabolic syndrome

The metabolic syndrome affects an estimated one million US adolescents. It is present in 30-50 per cent of overweight children. It is believed that the risk factors associated with the metabolic syndrome in childhood are precursors of cardiovascular disease that develops in adulthood. The primary cause is obesity leading to excess insulin production, which is associated with an increase in blood pressure and dyslipidemia (abnormal LDL and HDL blood levels). The most significant risk factor is the rate of increase in BMI. For overweight children and adolescents, for every half a unit increase in BMI, there's a corresponding 50 per cent increase in the risk of metabolic syndrome.

Type 2 diabetes

Type 2 diabetes (non-insulin dependant) typically presents in adolescents with a BMI greater then 30. In the US, just over four people in every 1000 have type 2 diabetes.

Type 2 diabetes is a progressive disease with no cure. Early intervention and diagnosis are paramount to minimising its long-term effects. If it's diagnosed early enough, the damage to the pancreas cells caused by the stress of excessive production of insulin can be minimised. However, once the damage is done it cannot be reversed.

The symptoms of type 2 diabetes can disappear, if you lose weight. This results in fat cells becoming less insulin resistant as they get smaller and an increase in the production of a beneficial hormone called adiponectin, which helps insulin to regulate blood glucose levels. Therefore weight management for obese children should be a primary goal.

However, though weight loss can help reduce type 2 diabetes symptoms, the results are not permanent and some people require insulin replacement therapy in the long-term. Monitoring and managing your symptoms are the keys to success. Characteristic symptoms of type 2 diabetes in the early phases of the disease are fatigue and excess production of urine.

Mental health and social issues

Overweight or obese children can experience significant mental health issues once they reach school age and are exposed to the inevitable taunting, teasing and bullying of playground culture. The effects can be catastrophic for some children. Depression, low self esteem, reduced self worth, poor body image, lower academic competence and difficulty with physical skills can become part of daily life. Without appropriate intervention the problem may well escalate, with the child likely to seek comfort in food, solace with inactivity and expression through misbehaviour.

The childhood rescue plan

To rescue a child from obesity, begin by considering six key areas:

1. The role of the parent: nurturer, manager and friend

2. Parental fears

3. Energy in versus energy out

4. Play, practise and exercise

5. Appetite and food management skills

6. Technology: the good the bad and the ugly

Think about these in relation to your children at the three different stages of their growing up: birth to preschool, primary school and high school.

The analogy of the airplane emergency is useful here: you must first put on your own oxygen mask, and then put on the child's. Set the example with leadership, provide the environment for change and encourage independence so your child can learn to take control.

The role of the parent: nurturer, manager and friend

Putting on your own oxygen mask before your child's requires you to look after yourself for the sake of your child. Your instinct may be to protect them first but you can only really do this if you take responsibility for the aspects of the situation and the environment you can control. Start the Rescue Me Flavour Diet and eFx program and learn to manage exercise, food and flavour. Set an example and establish a structure for your child to follow. Provide them with healthy behaviours to imitate from early on, so it's normal to grow up with fresh food and regular physical outings.

As a parent your relationship with your children continually evolves. This is particularly significant as your child moves from being dependent to independence. In stage 1 (birth to preschool) your main role is to nurture the growth of your child. During stage 2 (primary school) you may have to spend more time being a manager. During stage 3 (senior school), aim to develop a trust-based friendship. However recognise that you may have to play any one of these roles during all stages.

STAGE 1

In these early months and years, the child is nurtured mainly within the family, in the home environment. At this stage you're responsible for feeding your children and also for offering those opportunities that encourage the development of basic skills like walking, running, jumping and climbing. You set the home rules right from the start, providing rewards for good behaviour and discipline if behaviour is bad.

STAGE 2

Now you become more of a manager, as your child's time is shared between home, school and community activities. In each of these areas the child experiments with new physical skills, foods and social rules. Your job as a parent is to manage the child's growth and changes through these new experiences.

Be proactive in finding out how your children are influenced at school and in learning the counterbalancing or the complementary behaviours to promote when they come home. For example, find out what is served in the tuck shop at school, assess whether it's healthy or not and respond by adjusting the home diet or by changing your management of the money you give your child to spend at school to minimise their access to poor quality food.

Teachers and schools also have a discipline value system that they try to teach your children. You need to determine if the values they are teaching match what you expect at home and, if not, to decide how to manage the differences.

STAGE 3

Teenagers are able to explore a range of physical skills and food options. They are also dealing with issues such as peer pressure, self image, social values and information technology. A teenager has a growing sense of independence and with that independence comes responsibility, the partner of freedom.

If you continue to fulfill the roles of nurturer and manager during this time, you may deny your teenager the space they need to develop their identity, independence and capacity to deal with responsibility. It's hard to step back from these roles but try to let your relationship with your teenager evolve to one that's closer to friendship by the time they leave school.

It's essential to pass onto your teenagers the responsibility of choice: it's not possible, otherwise, for them to accept accountability for being overweight or unfit or for having unhealthy behaviours and values. You may need to let them fall a few times before they find their feet. This is what it means to be a friend. Don't get too close, but provide a sense of direction by setting an example, because what you do is fun and worthwhile.

Parental fears

On September 11, 2001 the word fear took on a new meaning. The world stood still for a moment and when it started moving again we were all more vigilant. Our lives, our families, our children became more precious. There are more security guards, more searches, more guns and more cause to watch our children more closely.

A child's opportunity to exercise is sometimes determined by the fear factor. How far away is the ball game? Is there transport? Is there supervision? Can a parent accompany the children? Do we trust the coach? Does the game finish after dark? Maybe the best option is not to go at all. Parental vigilance sometimes leads to children staying at home, where there's a small backyard (if there's any outdoor space at all) and not enough room to throw a basketball.

Do you drive your children everywhere, not let them walk home from school, keep them inside, give them a Nintendo to play with, let them watch more TV, surf the internet and eat what they like? Or do you replace these habits with new healthy ones?

If your child wants to play a team sport, then help them get safely to the game and back by establishing a car pool with parents you know. If they go to the park, teach them about road safety and other safety issues such as stranger danger. Set strict times for returning home, and ask them to go with a friend.

Weekends are great opportunities for families to exercise together, be it bike riding, tennis, swimming or any group sport. If your child has a weight problem then regular family exercise combined with the correct diet heads him or her in the right direction. Exercising together so your child is supervised by you is the perfect way to keep your child safe and get some exercise yourself at the same time.

Energy in versus energy out

Infancy is a time of amazing growth, reshaping, physical development and skill acquisition. To sustain this growth, your child's energy needs are high. However, you still have to know when your child is being

A child who sits in front of TV for hours on end eating potato chips and doughnuts is an ideal fat-storage machine.

fed too much or is doing too little. An infant, toddler or child can still become overweight.

Western countries have developed age-related BMI growth charts to help monitor your child's development, and these can easily be found on the internet. The average BMI changes significantly with age, rising sharply in infancy from approximately 11 at 35 weeks gestation to 18 at eight months and then falling during preschool years to 15.5. The BMI then steadily increases to 21 by the age of 18 years.

Regular checks of your child's weight with a community nurse can help determine what percentile they are in. If your infant's BMI is above the 85th percentile on the growth chart, be prepared to monitor their weight versus their height ratio more diligently over the next two years. As a baby's growth is so rapid, and the unique product of its medical, environmental and genetic circumstances, it takes this long to determine what the pattern of weight gain is and whether there is a problem.

Monitoring BMI between the ages of three to eight will give you a good idea as to whether the child is predisposed to obesity in adulthood. If your child's BMI is above the 95th percentile then they are considered obese. If they are in the 85th and 95th percentile, then you should seek out diet management, blood pressure and cholesterol assessments. Ongoing BMI check ups with community nurses, chemist, and doctors are important. The risk of not monitoring your children's health is too great, especially as the incidence of type 2 diabetes and metabolic syndrome increases.

Play, practise and exercise

Genetics is important, but the environment in which the child grows up can be the real driver in relation to weight gain. For example, irrespective of the parents' weight, children are less likely to become overweight if the parents are trained intensively in food and exercise management. With this in mind, realise that your physicality is not necessarily the same as your child's.

STAGE 1

There is no single right way for an infant to learn movement, which means they don't have to crawl before they walk. So now all you parents with bottom-scooting, commando-crawling infants can breathe a sigh of relief. The main thing is to provide the opportunities an infant needs to learn and practise crawling or walking and to monitor their ability to get better at it. This is the basis for the concept of interventional play, which every parent can do.

You can use interventional play to teach an infant 'stuck' in sitting how to get into a crawl position. Start with yourself seated on the floor with your legs in a wide 'v' position and the infant between your legs. Put some toys on the outside of your leg and encourage them to reach for the toys. With a little hands-on help with the positioning of their legs and rolling through their torso and pelvis your child will begin to manoeuvre itself into a crawl position over the leg to get to the toys. It may take a few repetitions of practise and a gradual reduction in the amount of hands-on assistance you do, but it is worth the effort. Try doing this on both sides as you may find the child is more efficient in one particular direction of movement. Once crawling, the child can more efficiently move around the room and develop leg strength in preparation for walking. The key to interventional play is to take an active role in practise, to be imaginative with how you play and to be present to make the environment safe. It takes some infants longer to develop leg strength or torso control than others. If you are concerned seek medical advice, but practise does make perfect so be persistent and keep it playful.

Childproof your house, stairs and cupboards because once you child gets moving they will really move.

It is when your baby grows into toddlerhood and then reaches preschool age that you should pay specific attention to the issue of obesity. At this point if your child is in the 85th to 95th percentile on the BMI growth chart, you should take extra steps to ensure they're developing the right movement and play behaviours for the future.

Continue to develop the concept of interventional play. This now may mean putting some time aside during play to practise specific skills like catching, kicking, walking distances or swimming. Buy or borrow toys or play equipment pitched at your child's developmental stage, to encourage skill development, practise through repetition and play. Reward achievement and the acquisition of new skills with general play, hugs, kisses, and vocal affirmation in your tone and words.

If not for them then do it for you. An overweight child who insists on being carried is a quick way to injure your back. Get them moving with interventional play and encourage practise of basic tasks like walking distances. Don't pick them up when they get tired – rather, try putting them on a push tricycle so they get a rest but still have their legs moving. You then get to push them, which is much safer for your back and allows you to get some exercise too.

Develop your awareness as to how long your child can concentrate on learning new skills such as catching a ball before they get distracted and run off to start chasing birds or ask to be carried. This may mean 10 minutes of catching practise then a return to general play. Keep it at that level for a while and if you feel like working on another skill, practise later in the day for the same amount of time. Once you are practicing several different skills at different times of the day, increase the time for practise to 15 minutes and so on as the child grows older.

Some libraries offer toy exchanges so that you can keep updating your children's playing opportunities.

STAGE 2

If your child is overweight and you've decided on the childhood rescue option, then - as you did with your own rescue - begin by identifying what's preventing them from exercising or playing so they can burn extra energy.

If it's skill level (for example they run poorly or seem clumsy), then just as you did with your rescue program, you must find the right skill level at which to start and move forward from there. Don't be afraid to practise skills with your child as it may surprise you how much you know about running, kicking, throwing, catching, hopping, climbing, jumping, dancing and rhythm. There are a lot of ball games you can invent that positively reinforce a successful catch with a progression to a more difficult one on the next attempt.

Explore your child's skill levels by adding new challenges or providing the right environment for success. The latter may mean getting a smaller baseball bat or cricket bat to make it easier for your child to learn to hit a ball. Get a smaller and lighter football, basketball or netball to practise kicking, passing and catching. If you play a game, keep the field small or get a basketball hoop at a height your children can throw the ball into.

The challenge is to believe you can make the difference. The most important thing is to take an interest in your child's skills and to remember to keep the practise regular. As you did with your eFx program, write down the skills you feel comfortable teaching and then find a point at which to start.

At primary school, the physical, intellectual and social skills your child is taught are determined by the syllabus and the school's ethos. But it is important to realise that probably many school teachers have limited physical skill knowledge and limited resources. Your child still needs your help.

Take an active role. Talk with the teacher, asking them what physical skills your child will be expected to learn during the term. Then try to help your child understand the rules of the games and practise the skill components. For example, if the school is teaching baseball or softball you can practise hitting and catching, or take the kids to professional games so they can learn the rules and get excited about the sport.

To help your child learn skills you don't feel confident in teaching or that the school syllabus doesn't cover, look for advice or find somewhere your child can learn them. There are many after-school groups or classes that teach children skills, from tennis to karate and beyond. Try to expose your children to a variety of activities to see which ones they like the most. Give them the opportunity and they will surprise you.

Remember, you are the example. If you practise your own rescue eFx then use the five Es (enjoyment, exertion, endurance, execution and evaluation) for your child's rescue as well.

Enjoyment is the first E, don't forget. It should be experienced by both you and your child.

Exertion is about making your child work at a level of intensity that causes them to puff.

Endurance is a bit tricky, as most children don't concentrate for long, so keep the practise and play moving at a good speed and offer frequent rests where they can talk about what they are trying to learn.

Execution requires creating the right environment and asking your child to work at the skill level appropriate to them. If you're unsure what this is, talk to your child's teacher and work on the skills taught at school.

Evaluate their success with a plan. Write it down, tell your friends, and get your child to talk about what being fit and mobile is all about. As your child reaches the end of junior school it is important to acknowledge their developing sense of independence and self image. Children by this stage will be well aware of their weight issues. The playground is not always a level playing field, and the way your child plays with other children can provide a good idea as to how their physical and social skills are affected by being overweight. It's not too soon to encourage responsible choice and an understanding of the concept of self management. Your children know, live and breathe the real big fat truth, and they too can choose a difference.

STAGE 3

Shoe sizes are going up, pimples have arrived, limbs get longer, bodies get clumsy, and appetites change.

High school years offer the not-to-be-missed opportunity to develop a trust-based friendship with your child and to nurture your child's growing independence. Encourage your teenager to take responsibility for weight management and to understand the necessity for exercise. Don't let them sacrifice exercise for academic studies, as the two complement each other. Teach your child about the five Es and ask them to start making choices and to write or draw a plan.

Enjoyment comes through ongoing participation, so if your teenager is uncomfortable with their current exercise program, look at alternatives. Being overweight or obese is not an excuse to avoid exercise or sport. There are a lot of sports where being larger is valued, such as rugby union, rugby league, football, athletics, boxing, rowing, dance and acrobatics. Encourage your teenager to investigate groups such as bush walking clubs, rock

CHAPTER 7 | CHILDHOOD OBESITY AND THE BIG FAT TRUTH

or the local gymnasium, as these offer great opportunities to develop skills in a variety of ways. Many offer activities appropriate for all levels of skill.

Exertion can be more fully explored. Teenagers can understand the concept of the BMI as a measure of weight. Teach them the Borg scale or make sure they know how to take a pulse. If you are on a walk with your teenager, ask them to tell you how hard they are working by getting them to rate their exertion level using the Borg scale (see chapter 3, page 38).

Endurance over a long exercise period may be hard for some overweight or obese teenagers. Introduce them to interval training, which requires bursts of activity rather then prolonged bouts of it. As your child becomes more confident, gradually build up the duration of the exercise bursts.

Execution can be challenging at some points of a teenager's life as their body may go through rapid periods of growth. This may result in the execution of physical skills taking a downward plunge. Someone who was the fastest runner or best kicker just can't seem to do it any more.

Encourage your child and keep them active so they don't fall into a downward spiral of low self esteem and withdrawal from physical activity. Remind them that enjoying exercise takes practise and patience. If your child is interested in developing specific skills then encourage them: if you can't get access to advice or coaching, pick up a book or get onto the internet to learn more.

Evaluation comes to the fore. Exercise needs to be more then a lifestyle choice - it is a necessity. Evaluating successful outcomes is essential to set the right behaviours for the future. If your teenager is obese then monitor their BMI, blood pressure and blood sugar levels regularly. The threat of type 2 diabetes is real. Work with teachers and health professionals to get a teenager eFx plan into action. Accountability is important for success, so make it relevant using technology like blogs, e-mail and text SMS or video.

Appetite and food management

It all begins before birth. A mother's weight, diet, social habits such as smoking and alcohol intake all influence her child's birth weight. Underweight babies need feeding and overweight babies require monitoring. Demand feeding may result in fat babies if the breastmilk is high in fat and the feeds are too frequent. If the baby is healthy it's time to teach them a routine by feeding them at regular intervals, according to the advice you're given by your early childhood nurse. Fat babies can develop into fat toddlers.

Voice control as exercised by parents is little taught and even less understood. From the moment of birth, a baby's cognitive skills develop rapidly. The baby absorbs and stores information like a sponge, much of it learnt from observing your behaviour. In order to introduce routine with breastfeeding and sleep times, use a distinct change in your vocal tone so that the baby distinguishes sleep periods from waking; feeding time from non-feeding time and so on. When the parent's voice is low, slow and soothing it's sleep time. When the voice is louder, happier and more playful it's wake time and so on. It's simple for you to set a pattern and stick to it.

From the age of six months, children will develop their eating patterns according to the lifestyle of their family. Three meals, six meals, snacks, good habits or bad, the children will follow suit. So this is when you must start developing good habits with healthy food and remember: routine routine routine.

From the age of six months many babies are ready for solid foods. Babies progressing from breast milk or formula to solids will develop a sweet tooth if given the chance. When adding stewed fruit to cereal, don't add sugar, just a pinch of salt will bring out the flavour in the fruit.

Don't give babies juice; water can be introduced to babies very early in life. In their first year make sure the water is boiled and that bottles are sterilised.

From about six months on, babies can benefit from the vitamins and minerals in boiled and mashed vegetables. This can be an introduction to a love for vegetables throughout their life. Boil the vegetables in a small amount of water and mash them into some of the same water for full nutritional benefits.

Children can assist with the tasks involved in preparing meals from quite a young age: setting the table, helping to wash, peel or chop vegetables, preparing other foods and certainly, once they're a bit older, washing the dishes or stacking the dishwasher. They can help make tricky foods such as homemade pasta (even though it may mean covering themselves with flour in the process).

Involving children in this way can generate an interest in food to the point where even a young child can be involved in making menu decisions. It lays good foundations for discussions about and management of food choices later on.

As far as possible, feed all of the family the same foods, making allowances for special needs such as a teenager who does a lot of sport. Discourage eating dinner in front of the television. This practise encourages a sedentary lifestyle that encourages a lack of activity and communication with other family members in the home. 'What did you do today?' when sitting around the dinner table can be the catalyst not only for friendly conversation but also for planning the next day or weeks. Sadly, the healthy practise of dinnertime family conversation is in many households a long-lost tradition.

Ideas for hungry toddlers and babies with teeth

Easy finger food lunches can be quick to prepare and are also excellent for teaching dexterity and self-feeding techniques.

SUMMER LUNCH | Wheat crackers, crisp rice cakes, dried fruits, carrot sticks and cold skinless chicken.

WINTER LUNCH | Fried brown rice containing free range eggs scrambled in some olive oil and some lean ham or chicken, tossed with fresh chopped shallots and a dash of sesame oil. Add in green beans sometimes for extra crunch.

EVENING MEAL | This recipe is low in fat, high in protein and suitable for children 10 months of age and over.

Chicken and Vegetables

(Makes 4 medium size or 8 small servings)
1 large chicken breast, no skin
½ tablespoon light olive oil
1 small carrot, sliced
1 small potato, peeled and sliced
1 small zucchini, sliced
100g/3-4oz pumpkin, cubed
½ cup low fat milk
1 knob unsalted butter

Chop the chicken and gently stir fry in the oil over a moderate heat until cooked through. Cover and simmer for 10 minutes, adding a little water if too dry.
Divide into 4 (or 8) servings.

Boil all the vegetables until soft (6-8 minutes). Mash until very smooth, adding the milk and the butter.

Serve the chicken and the mashed vegetables together for toddlers 12-14 months and over. You can blend the chicken and the vegetables together for younger children with few teeth. Serve warm.

Reminder: chop the chicken to size depending on the age of the child and the number of teeth they have. Freeze in ice cube trays for easy, quick lunches for at-home toddlers. Add a slice of bread and a glass of milk and you have nutritious meals at your fingertips.

TODDLER SNACKS | This is the danger area. Allowing a grizzly, tired child to satisfy themselves with a snack bar or candy will lead to a disastrous habit. Have peeled carrots handy in the fridge along with apple or pear which can be offered as a snack if the child needs it. Sometimes a grizzly child is thirsty or tired and not hungry at all. Give them half an apple, a glass of water and a sleep and they will keep their hunger for the next scheduled meal. Avoid fruit juice and sugar drinks! Water, water, water!

A UK obesity study which observed 39 children aged between two and four and a half years over a 48 hour period found that 72.5 per cent didn't drink plain water. Excess intake of fruit juices and sugar drinks was found to have two opposite effects. The first is a failure to thrive, probably because such drinks don't provide the nutrients a child needs but also reduce the child's appetite for healthier food options.

The other is excessive weight gain due to excess energy intake. Fifteen per cent of the children in the study obtained their recommended daily carbohydrate intake through the sweet drinks and juices alone, yet 88 per cent of the mothers were happy with their children's drinking habits. Could this reflect the misconception responsible for many parents giving their children juice to drink: that juice is a healthy option?

Munch crunch lunch

Start your child's day with carbohydrates, protein and vitamins. Cereal and milk can create the basis of a child's breakfast. Offer a banana (especially on cooked oats) and a glass of diluted orange juice, milk or water. Add a slice of toast with jam or honey and you have a breakfast that will give a child of any age the energy they need to learn, exercise and arrive at lunchtime feeling well but ready for another meal.

If children are taking part in sporting programs (swimming, rugby, rowing or similar) a breakfast high in protein with some carbohydrates is required - egg, toast and fruit juice is a great way to start their day.

Think about freshness and balance when planning the midday meal, which the children eat out of your sight. School-bought lunches don't always provide a well balanced option as there are plenty of unwise choices to be made when parents are not looking. If possible, pack a sandwich with cold meats and crunchy salad. Make sure you consult with the child as to which salad they DON'T like and make a serious attempt to give them what they WILL eat, as otherwise the lunch will be given away or thrown in the garbage.

A piece of fruit and a drink bottle with diluted apple or orange juice (20 per cent juice and 80 per cent water) gives balance to the meal. Popcorn with no added salt or butter can be a great snack along with dry crackers and a handful of almonds. If your child is carrying a few extra pounds then they need to develop a taste for a munch crunch lunch, eating portioned fresh food from home.

A TASTY LUNCH BOX MEAL | Make a cold packed salad of steamed skinless chicken sliced up and tossed with a little tomato, Spanish onion jam and shredded iceberg lettuce. Add in some finely sliced sourdough Melba toast.

Your child can help put this lunch together and make the Melba toast themselves the evening before. Lightly toast up thinly sliced sourdough bread. Add nothing!

AFTER-SCHOOL SNACK | After-school treats can be a hazard for school age children. Keep them safe with this easy-to-make do-it-themselves drink.

Walnut Smoothie

1 cup orange juice
1 cup frozen chunks of mango
½ cup chopped walnuts
⅓ cup tofu (about 2 inch cube)

Place orange juice, mango, walnuts and tofu in the blender. Blend on low speed until ingredients start to mix together. Then increase to high speed and blend until smooth. Pour into glasses and sprinkle with walnuts. Can make up to 1 hour ahead. Serve with straw or spoon.

EVENING MEALS | An excellent low fat tasty meal for children (and teenagers) with a weight problem is cooked brown rice fried up in a little vegetable oil with a broken egg. Steamed fresh fish fillet with wilted English spinach or broccoli tossed in garlic and served on the rice will deliver a flavoursome, nutritious meal that can become a weekly favourite.

Training up teens

The kitchen is a place where you can do a great deal to guide your teenager towards independence. If children want different meals and as a family you decide to change to a healthier diet then give them a role in preparing the food. You may get them to cook once a week on a regular basis. Give them a selection of ingredients to choose from and then stand back. Supervise but give space - which may mean burnt pans, excessive flavour hits or bland food. If they want tasty food they have to learn to cook. It doesn't happen overnight but it does need to happen before they leave home because the alternative is fast, convenient foods and bad habits that are hard to beat.

AN EVENING MEAL | This can be fun for the kids to prepare and cook themselves, either on a weeknight or as a weekend barbecue.

Barbecue Beef & Chicken with Vegetable Kebabs

(Serves 4)

½ kg / 1.1lbs lean ground beef
1 egg
1 brown onion, finely diced
1 carrot, peeled and grated
4 chicken legs, skin removed
1 tablespoon light soy sauce
1 tablespoon olive oil

Kebabs

1 red bell pepper
1 green bell pepper
½ red onion
½ fresh pineapple
8 wooden skewers, soaked in cold water for 1 hour

Prepare the meat: mix the ground beef, egg, onion and carrot together and form into four hamburgers. Use wet hands to make it easier to mould them. Set aside in the fridge while you prepare the rest of the meal. Rinse the chicken legs under a running tap and pat dry. Place in a shallow bowl and pour the soy sauce over. Cover and refrigerate while you prepare the kebabs.

For the kebabs: wash, peel and trim the vegetables and pineapple into chunky pieces as similar in size as possible. Thread them alternately onto the skewers, almost filling the length of the wood.

To cook: clean the barbecue, heat and brush with the olive oil. Cook the chicken first and when cooked half through add on the hamburgers, then the kebabs. If using an open flame be very careful not to burn the kebabs as they only need a minute or two to remain tasty and juicy.

Don't spoil the meal with bread. Rely on the flavours of the meat, marinade, vegetables and fruit to deliver a fun and healthy meal. If you need more quantity simply add in a crispy green salad.

Technology - the good the bad and the ugly

The Z generation of today is very familiar with information technology and the ease of access it offers to instant gratifications, information, and the capacity to explore virtual worlds. It is amazing to watch a child smile in front of a digital camera and then ask immediately for it to be turned around so they can see themselves in the photo. The results are instant, and the decision is made on the spot to keep or dispose of the photo. Undeniably, technology offers great advances with regard to education and access to knowledge. But it's also undeniable that this technology brings with it some not so positive consequences for the quick fix, channel flicking generation of the future.

The opportunity to sit and be entertained for hours at a time in front of a screen can lead to the couch potato phenomenon. To prevent this occurring you need to help your children enjoy technology as an accessory, not a necessity. Information technology is an essential cog in the way contemporary society works and shielding your children from it entirely is neither possible nor desirable. Rather, get back to the basics: teach moderation and set quotas for time spent in front of the screen. Put the television and computer in common areas, and not in children's bedrooms. Flick off the technology switch and jump into exercise and play.

This may be a hard behaviour to promote immediately so start slowly. Talk to your child and set rules about using the computer and television. Determine how much time they currently spend sitting in a chair in front of a computer or TV screen, then set a timetable to reduce the amount by 20 per cent every two weeks. Plan activities to use the time differently, such as playing with toys or providing sports equipment they can use in the back yard or take to the park with a friend. Be proactive. Get involved.
Make a difference. Shape the future.

The problem is obesity. The solution is you.

Chapter 8
Baby boomers - a new lease of life

Chapter 8: Baby boomers - a new lease of life

Over the past 20 years there has been an 18 per cent increase in obesity among the over 65s and today, 48 per cent of baby boomers are either overweight or obese. There is no way to turn back the clock, but there are things boomers can do to reduce the risks associated with being overweight. You are at a stage in your life now when you can take a step back and consider your options. Whether married, single or with a partner, the next few decades of your life can be some of the most interesting. The kids have left home, retirement is an option and health should become a priority.

It's your time now

It's not until you retire that you fully realise the degree to which your work life was integrated into your everyday existence. Before, when you had a conversation with an acquaintance it's likely the question 'How's work?' was readily asked. Work and its associated projects provided ways to relate to those around you.

Once work is removed, quite a gap may appear. This becomes filled with leisure, family and, if inclined, community roles or activities. It can mean suddenly spending many more hours with your partner, at home or discovering new ways to occupy your time. During your working years, leisure seemed to be the light at the end of the endless tunnel - and then you realise that now there is no tunnel! Don't miss this opportunity. Use it to set a new course in life.

Hours and years at work condition the body for specific physical activities, be it sitting or standing for long periods or doing a particular physical task. However, your time spent in industry may also have de-conditioned or de-trained your body when it comes to simple leisure activities like walking, running, swimming or general gardening. This is particularly likely due to the increasingly sedentary nature of work, where the chair and computer are king. The consequence of a long working life spent mainly at a computer could be lower back pain, neck pain, tight and weak postural and dynamic muscles and, of course, weight gain. The patterning of work also encourages certain eating, drinking and social habits.

All of which suddenly arrive at a moment of change - retirement.

The good news is that all those skills you developed at work can now be put to use on the project called ME! And the Rescue Me eFx program and Flavour Diet are a great way to start. You're never too old to learn, so why not become involved in social activities that require physical skill and developing dexterity.

For some people, this may mean joining walking groups, going to mature move fitness classes, going to the gym, bike riding or learning to dance. It's a time to rediscover your sense of play, fun and time for sex - ooops… don't let the kids hear you say that; they still think they invented it. Oh yes, the rescue of your eSx life should be a thought worth considering. It would be nice not to have a big belly or a backache or hip problem getting in the way of your enjoyment - of 'retirement', that is.

In fact for those baby boomers who are yet to retire, it is worth adopting the Rescue Me approach before you get there. If you are in a partnership and one of you has retired they can get started on the program quicker. Make sure your working partner has plenty of opportunity to become jealous of what you are doing so they can join in the fun when it comes to their turn.

The family home an empty nest

For years you nurture and manage the family. When children are young, you teach them to catch and hit a ball, tie their own shoes, fix their own lunches and, eventually, how to cook, drive the family car and do their own laundry. You spend time teaching them in the hope they will become independent, productive young adults. And wasn't this the goal?

However, some parents have conflicting feelings when the kids begin to venture out on their own, off to school, interstate or overseas. The father may want to convert the empty bedroom into a study while the mother would like to keep it unaltered for holiday time. Mum's feelings may include a sense of uselessness. She finds herself wondering what to do with the time once spent chauffeuring and attending school functions.

If parents are married, this time can be used to focus on each other. It can be an amazing time to renew the intimacy you once shared and to concentrate on your relationship. Whether part of a couple or a single parent, there are many ways to lessen the feelings of loss when the nest is emptied.

For many years you may have focused your attention on the direction and wellbeing of the family. Any extra time after work was spent looking after the needs of others. Just as finishing work leaves a gap to fill, as the children leave home you're left with an empty spot that needs reshaping.

At first it may be hard to refocus your attention but it should return to you. Hours in the car driving teenagers to activities, doing their washing, cooking and general management may have left you without the time and energy to exercise and to manage food for yourself. In particular, it may have been hard to manage your portion sizes and food preferences when you have a growing son with 'hollow legs' who demands bigger servings. But now you may no longer have someone who stands at the open fridge door scanning for the slightest bit of food to eat. Your food bill plummets - so take the opportunity to restock your fridge with quality food that can enhance the flavour of your cooking and be easily portioned.

Many baby boomers are grandparents. The wheel of life rotates around one further click and you are now in the position of advisor to these new lives coming up through the family. Grandparents can be detached enough to provide advice that complements the efforts of parents, but don't undervalue your role in helping set the right behaviours for health management. Grandparents who exercise regularly, live a loving life and eat healthily set a wonderful example for their family. Grandparents who come for a visit can also promote healthy food choices and not just arrive with treats like cupcakes and candy. They must play a major role in the fight against childhood obesity where they can.

Leisure, where time is precious and freedom to move is priceless

When you've retired from work and/or the children have left home, you have a lot more leisure time. You may choose to travel, joining the cavalcade of 'grey nomads'. With travel comes the freedom of new experiences and places but also hours spent sitting and driving and the loss of routine. Even very health conscious people may find this break in routine leads to eating too much convenience food and little or no exercise.

If this is you then maybe it's time to reconsider the notion of travel. Think of it not as destination-driven but as journeying for health. Making health a priority may mean slowing the journey down and incorporating new activities and destinations that may be a little off the 'beaten track'. To maintain your eFx program, visit places with bush walks or beach walks. Take advantage of the scenery and pack some good food to eat to match the view. A cup of tea, bottle of wine, or a barbecue tastes much better after a walk in beautiful surroundings.

If you have the room and the equipment, then strap some bikes onto the car, caravan or recreational vehicle and take some time out for bike riding. Cycling is a worldwide sport, and there are plenty of options for riding routes. On Lord Howe Island in Australia, cycling is the main way to get around. No cars allowed. Those who are uncomfortable riding a traditional

Abalone with garlic, ginger and chili

Remove the abalone from the shell. Clean, and then soften by hitting the centre muscle firmly a few times with a hammer. Rinse. Roll in plain flour. Heat light vegetable oil in a pan on the barbecue until hot, then add garlic, ginger and hot dry chili. Add abalone and cook for one minute.

Serve with salad and a glass of cool white wine.

Take your barbecue down to the beach - throw in a line and pull in some local seafood, light up the barbecue and splash on some olive oil; open a bottle and seize the day!

RESCUE me

166

two-wheeler might try a tricycle. What a great way to preserve the environment and encourage exercise.

Food lovers might plan a journey organised around an understanding of flavour and the regional influences on food and wine.

Fresh, regional and seasonal

If you are travelling in Western Australia and heading south, the Margaret River region is well worth a visit. Boutique wineries are scattered in beautiful countryside where you can also find fresh, regional produce in farmers' markets and numerous cafes and restaurants. This coastal area is famous for cabernet merlot and semillon sauvignon blanc blends.

Taking the motor home across the Nullarbor to South Australia will reward you with amazing, unique scenery and more wineries than you can count. If you venture high into the Adelaide Hills you will find cool climate wines where sauvignon blanc is one of the favourites. The red soil of Coonawarra offers great cabernets and further south McLaren Vale produces a stunning range of shiraz.

If you are looking for a great pinot noir, beautiful bush walks and mountains of home grown fruit then leave the motor home on the mainland and hop across to Tasmania.

Take a day trip to the Hunter Valley where the fresh young semillon, regional cheese, and locally made chocolates are hard to resist.

Move it or lose it with OA and obesity

Osteoarthritis, or OA, is a degenerative joint disease affecting 15 per cent of the population. It is often characterised by pain, loss of joint mobility, muscular de-conditioning, detraining, reduced functional ability and postural changes. It affects the load-bearing cartilage tissue in joints and the surrounding bone and soft tissue. The damage may be caused by both inflammatory and biomechanical factors.

The chance of developing osteoarthritis increases with age and obesity is a major risk factor. Obesity may contribute to the onset of OA in both weight-bearing joints such as knee and hips and in non-weight-bearing joints such as hands or wrists. Obviously, the more unnecessary weight you carry the greater the loads and stress through the joints. Less obvious is that the risk of developing OA is increased by inflammatory reactions associated with the metabolic syndrome and by being sedentary.

Metabolic syndrome associated with obesity can be like a shadow that gets bigger as your body get bigger. The inflammatory components of the metabolic syndrome that are released from abdominal fat cells (adipose tissue) into the bloodstream are called adipokines. They can accelerate the breakdown of cartilage of both weight and non-weight bearing joints.

If you have OA you may have to take that extra step to find the right exercise to suit you. The main thing is to make a start.

OA may be degenerative but the worst thing to do is stop moving. You really have to move it or you will lose it. Moving the joints at a steady flowing pace can help regenerate the joint and improve its range. But it takes time because cartilage is very slow growing and has a poor blood supply. It is essential to get the joints moving as the muscles need to be strengthened to support your joint. Exercising may be painful but it is worth the effort. A physical therapist can help you retrain your movement patterns to avoid those causing the pain or excessive wear and tear. Some simple and well directed tips can make all the difference.

If you suffer from OA and want to do the Rescue Me eFx program, then the pool is one of the best places to start. Your buoyancy in the water allows you to move more freely so you can put your joints through a variety of ranges. If your knees or hips are affected, first find a heated pool that you can get in and out of comfortably and safely. Start with a small amount of walking and maybe more noodle work, especially deep water cycling and leg press to develop your leg strength (see chapter 4 for details). If you want to lose weight, don't forget to keep your exertion levels up by rotating between leg and upper torso work. Your legs may hurt but you still have the rest of the body to work with.

A foot massage for the one you love is similar to a good glass of champagne - anywhere - any time!

Gyrotonic exercises on the pulley tower and studio Pilates exercises on the reformer (see chapter 4) are similar to pool exercises but on land. These two unique exercise systems can help retrain the biomechanics of your knees, hips, pelvis and spine. The exercises are cyclical, which is favourable for joint reconditioning, and can be well controlled and tailored to suit your body by the practitioner.

Menopause and an increasing waist line

Why on earth it's called 'Men'opause and not 'women'opause is not clear. It is clear however that at this time in their lives, women are at an increased risk of weight gain leading to obesity and therefore increased risk of the metabolic syndrome, type 2 diabetes and cardiovascular disease (CVD).

Post-menopause status increases the risk of metabolic syndrome by 60 per cent. It has been found that 16 per cent of pre-menopause women are insulin resistant and when combined with menopause the chances of developing metabolic syndrome increases. The increase in the prevalence of metabolic syndrome in women after menopause may also explain why the risk that women will develop CVD catches up to that for men in this age group.

Female baby boomers need to be aware that the prevalence of obesity in adult women rises significantly each decade, until it begins tapering off later in life. In particular, the years surrounding menopause are associated with dangerous weight gain. On average, it appears that women gain about 1lb/0.5 kg per year during this time. It is worth realising that in post-menopause women it is waist circumference not BMI that predicts cardiovascular risk factors.

Because the factor most consistently related to weight gain in this age-group is decreased physical activity, menopausal women (that's you, baby boomers) must make the choice to adopt an exercise program for the remaining years of their lives.

High blood pressure

30 per cent of people who have high blood pressure (hypertension) also suffer from metabolic syndrome. Obese people who have metabolic syndrome, including hypertension, even without type 2 diabetes, can be regarded as being in a state of accelerated vascular aging. Their blood pressure will be higher due to an increase in the level of activation of the sympathetic nervous system. The impact of this system that causes a fright, flight or fight response in the body may be responsible for increasing the risk of CVD.

Food choices for a healthier you

In addition to seeking medical advice you can instigate a self-help program through careful exercise and diet planning. Omega-3 fish oil may help prevent CVD, artheriosclerosis and strokes. Including fresh deep sea fish in your diet regularly will help you obtain these oils.

Also, antioxidants such as vitamin E in combination with vitamin C are valuable in preventing damage by free radicals to your general tissues and arteries. You can find these nutrients and more in vegetable oils, nuts, green leafy vegetables like cabbage and citrus fruits.

Resveratrol is one of the main antioxidants found in wine. It is a phenolic bioflavonoid compound which acts as an antifungal agent in grapes, especially during ripening. Dr Edwin Frankel, of Davis University in California, has shown that these antioxidants in wine are five times more potent than the benchmark antioxidant, vitamin E.

Celery is a high source of silicon which may also be beneficial in combating OA and is a good appetite suppressor. You can have it fresh as a snack, cooked in stocks for soups or even as a substitute for onion in stir fries or pasta dishes.

Fresh lemons in tea, on salads and grilled on the barbeque are a good source of vitamin C as will as adding tasty flavour to meals. Try this method of preserving lemons for taking away on holiday or simply adding to the pantry.

A simple use of preserved lemons is to fry chicken pieces on both sides in a pan, then throw in the sliced zest of one piece of preserved lemon, with a splash of white wine (or vegetable stock) and some kalamata olives, to add moisture and finish cooking through. A little dried thyme would be the preferred herb to add, if you like.

This method of including lemons in your diet is a favourite of French-born Florence Stratham. She and her husband Richard and their family have an organic vineyard and olive grove in Canowindra in western New South Wales on the east coast of Australia.

Baby boomers are aging and getting bigger. It is a time in your life when you can still make a difference to yourself and others and see the benefits of that change reflected onto future generations.

Lemon and lime ideas

If the fruit is a little hard roll it firmly up and down on a flat surface to soften before cutting.

Cut one or two in half and place face down on the barbecue or grill. Brown their faces a little and use for decorating and flavouring the dish.

Lemon and lime juice plus some halved fruit in a jug of iced water at meal time. No need for sugar.

Squeeze over hot pasta as an alternative to regular sauces. A little fresh chili and black pepper and you have a gourmet meal.

Barbecued or pan fried lemon and limes become much juicier and easier to squeeze.

Preserved lemons

Lemons (not waxed or chemically sprayed)
Sea salt
Bay leaf
Lemon juice

Quarter the lemons and pack in a sterile jar alternating each layer with salt. Add a bay leaf, cover the lemons with extra lemon juice and keep for 4 weeks before opening the jar. Will store in cupboard for 4 to 5 months, but refrigerate after opening.

Chapter 9
The balancing act of chronic back pain and obesity

Chapter 9: The balancing act of chronic back pain and obesity

Irrespective of which comes first, obesity and pain can join forces and create multiple problems. Finding a solution can often be like a fine balancing act: managing pain symptoms and reduced mobility and understanding that you have to exercise to lose weight despite the pain. Pain and obesity will conspire to prevent you from tackling either issue. The solution may take time and require specific pacing of your individual eFx program.

To set the right pace, you have to learn how to determine your limits and then build up your body's strength so you can uncouple these problems. Chronic pain demands patience, knowledge, the right timing for exercise progression and the appropriate environment and exercise system for success.

Lower back pain and the signal to change

In western society 80 per cent of the population will experience lower back pain (LBP) at some stage in life. At any point in time about 5.5 per cent of the American population will be experiencing an episode of pain. There is currently an exponential increase in chronic disability associated with lower back pain. People who are already obese and are experiencing LBP are likely to suffer more significant physical disability and an increased chance of it becoming chronic.

Obesity may also mean that LPB is more likely to occur. For example, women who are obese at age 23 have a significantly increased chance of developing the condition at age 32 -33 years. Often, however, the issue of obesity and LBP can be a bit like the chicken and the egg. Both can be associated with reduced physical conditioning and detraining. And as with obesity, a passive attitude to the management of LBP - such as 'My back hurts; I need to lie down and rest" may be extremely detrimental.

Though it can be disabling, pain can also be seen as a trouble signal sent by your body, urging you to change your current life style. Obesity and LBP may develop as a consequence of bad personal management decisions made while balancing life's demands and expectations. A well structured plan is required in order to get on top of these problems.

There are three main types of LBP:

1. Simple or non-specific LBP, where the pain is isolated to the lower back.

2. Referred LBP, where the symptoms are both in the back and in the lower extremities of the body such as the buttocks, legs or feet.

3. Neurological LBP, which involves a disc protrusion encroaching on the sciatic or femoral nerves. This third type impacts on muscle strength and sensations in the legs due to reduced input from the nerve. In severe cases it can even affect bladder function, in which case an emergency surgical procedure may be required.

LBP management

These three types of pain can require very different kinds of management. In particular, simple and referred LBP in the acute form often improve quickly, with 80 per cent of sufferers being able to return to work in two to three weeks.

However, they become much more complex to manage if they progress into their sub-acute form, which persists up to six months, and beyond that into chronic LBP. The cause of these two types of LBP can vary, from small tears in the disc, aggravation of the transverse process joints in the spine, muscle de-conditioning, de-training and muscular imbalances to pelvic dysfunction, degeneration - and the list goes on.

Neurological LBP requires very specific management right from the start and expectations for recovery should be slower. This form of LBP is relatively rare, but the disc protrusions that characterise it are more common in obese people. Symptoms may include muscle weakness and sensation loss as the legs do not receive effective messages from the brain. This will mean that walking may be difficult, with a sense of giving way or wobbly legs.

When experiencing neurological symptoms it's important to unload the spine and to take the weight off the disc that is putting pressure on the nerves. Treatment may involve direction-specific exercises to help alleviate the pain and symptoms caused by the disc pushing on and aggravating the nerve. Exercises in the pool using your body's buoyancy to relieve the compression load on the disc can be excellent.

It's very easy to gain excess weight in this situation, due to your limited ability to move and therefore to burn energy.

Neurological LBP, weight gain and eFx in action

As a result of a lifting accident a 35 year old professional woman developed a bulging disc in her lower back, which pushed on the sciatic nerve causing neurological left leg weakness and numbness. She was 165lb/75kg before the injury and had been standing and walking at work for 10 hour stretches, four days a week. She had difficulty going to work and with reduced mobility her weight ballooned out to 255lb/116kg.

The woman required surgical management as her pain and weakness due to nerve compression became worse. With a weakening leg and an increasing body weight her situation looked bad. Following surgery, however, her leg symptoms began to improve. She embarked on an exercise regimen that involved a graded Pilates studio home program three or four times a week and, on weekends, a pool program with plenty of walking in the water.

In four months she lost 64lbs/29kg and was determined to lose the last 26lbs/12kg to return to her pre-injury weight. Returning from an injury and surgery such as this, it was important for her to start at the right place and find the movements she was comfortable doing. She could then gradually develop her abilities from that point.

Chronic LBP

Those who have chronic LBP would be very familiar with the many descriptions of their problem. It seems that you can get a different reason for your pain every time you walk into a new therapist's clinic. At some point you may start to wonder: 'Is it all in my head?' - particularly when CT and MRI scans reveal no definitive cause of your problem.

What may be even worse, however, is when these investigations and clinicians do find a problem, which then becomes the label for all of the symptoms of your LBP. Unfortunately, treating chronic LBP may not be a simple cause and effect relationship. Does this sound familiar? It's a little like obesity and the notion that losing weight can be described as a simple matter of eating a little less and exercising a little more. Remember Bob's thoughts on weight loss in chapter 2?

Unraveling the obesity and chronic LBP conspiracy

When chronic LBP and obesity conspire together, you have to work much harder to stop the trajectory towards increased pain, reduced function and weight gain. What you need is a solidly structured approach to your pain and weight management.

Of course it is important to see a clinician who can evaluate both the anatomical and psychological aspects of your pain. There you go – it's been said: the psychological nature of pain. Don't be afraid of this word. It's not dirty and it doesn't mean you have a psychological problem. In fact, the more you understand how fear, depression, anxiety, and stress contribute to your problem, the better your chance of developing a plan to prevent it becoming worse. As with an understanding of obesity, understanding pain can involve considering the influence of your work environment and the values or expectations of people around you.

In managing chronic LBP, whether simple or referred, exercising while in pain does not always mean you are causing damage to your back. Seek advice to learn how to work with your pain so you can improve muscle strength, posture and endurance and start to counter the disability that chronic LBP causes in your life.

Pain reshaping you

Being normal and happy to sit at work for eight hours a day can quickly change when LBP enters your life. You may find that walking to work, sitting comfortably for longer then 10 minutes, or even bending down to pick an item up off the floor can become a major effort. These experiences can be very humbling and sometimes scary.

What if

You are 390lb/180kg and you have diabetes, kidney stones and chronic pain in your knees, hips and back. Do you buy an electronic motor scooter and spin around the park in that? Or do you seek advice and continue to take even short walks, in an attempt to improve your condition?

You are 100lb/45kg overweight, have pain from your back shooting down your leg and are experiencing problems getting up and down the stairs. Do you sell the house and purchase a single story home or do you lose weight, improve your fitness and keep the house?

How to make a difference

Through professional, medical and/or sports-related guidance you can learn to stop the process of de-conditioning and de-training associated with loss of function. The Rescue Me eFx program and Flavour Diet can step you in the right direction to help reduce your chronic pain.

To design an eFx program that will assist with both weight loss and LBP you may have to consider some additional steps to those outlined in chapters 3 and 4.
These may include:

1. **Seeking medical advice** to establish the appropriate level and type of movement to get your body moving in the right direction. Choosing the right exercise system that supports your body may involve some trial and error. Be patient.

2. **Adapting the exercises** in Chapter 4 specifically for you. In fact some exercises may aggravate your pain if introduced incorrectly too early and or done too often.

Even the basic exercises may be too advanced for your rehabilitation program, so proceed with caution.

3. **Determining how comfortable you are** with the duration of your exercise session and reduce it by 20 per cent in order to protect your condition from any aggravation. If you're comfortable exercising for short periods such as 10 minutes, then you may consider doing two or three eight minute sessions with a rest between each one. Do this three or four times a week and slowly build up the duration and frequency as you start seeing results.

Adapting and troubleshooting your eFx program to help LBP

Pilates exercises offer benefits in training the deep abdominal muscles which help to support your spine. However, some of the basic Pilates eFx mat exercises such as roll ups and rolling may be too advanced in the beginning. Studios and clinicians may offer pre-Pilates or torso stability classes that can progress you nicely into the basic Pilates eFx exercises. If you're uncomfortable working on the floor or even on your back, Pilates studios are worth a visit to see if training on a reformer or a waunda chair can get you moving more effectively.

For those who are uncomfortable on the floor or whose work involves sitting at a computer, Gyrokinesis is a great option. With Gyrokinesis your chair doesn't just provide you with somewhere to sit, but with an opportunity for exercise as well. In the chair you can practise arch and curl, twist, side bends and the wave. However, even more important is remembering to get up and walk around regularly as our bodies are not designed to sit for eight hours a day, five days a week.

A good guide for the prevention of back pain is to remember that for every hour you sit at a desk you should do five minutes of exercise. Therefore an eight hour day at a desk requires 40 minutes of exercise. Look upon it as a debt you owe your body. If you can't train sufficiently during the week, then pay your exercise debt on the weekend.

People for whom walking is difficult due to pain, particularly that caused by neurological LBP, will find the pool or the bike suits them much better. If you are experiencing a lot of pain then try walking in the pool in chest high water, sometimes with two floatation noodles under your arms. The noodles will provide gentle traction to your spine, helping to release muscular tension and possible compression on injured discs. You can do some very good interval work both in the pool and on the bike to help you on your weight loss journey. Interval training (see chapter 3, page 39) involves a regular change of speed in your activity.

Fear of movement

Not all disability associated with chronic LBP is due to pain. Fear avoidance to prevent an episode of pain can be the major factor preventing you from doing activities.

At first this may be slight avoidance, such as not reaching up to put a box on a high shelf because it hurts to lift the box above shoulder height. This fear may lead you to delegate the task to someone else. One way to help overcome this fear is by practising the components that make up the movement. This is where the gym eFx program comes into play.

To gain confidence in lifting the box, start with building leg strength, by doing leg extensions and machine leg press. To develop arm strength for reaching above the head, start with shoulder blade and upper torso strengthening with seated rows and lat pull downs. Keep the weight low and repetitions high (15 at maximum) to begin with. Progress your weight up slowly each two weeks for six to 12 weeks.

Once you feel comfortable with this then you may progress to barbell lifts, bicep curls and military press. It is a good idea to use just the bar and no additional weights for two weeks. If you experience a breakdown in technique and form and find that you're doing compensatory movements, this is the cue to stop.

Over the next six weeks you may progressively add weights. Next try picking dumbbells off the floor and then lifting them above your head, to simulate the full task you previously avoided at work. All these exercises will gradually build your limb and torso strength, co-ordination and awareness of technique and form.

Component training like this will help you to develop sufficient strength to lift boxes above the head again, with less fear of back pain. The message here is don't avoid physical tasks. Rather than deleting them from your daily life, explore ways to build the skills you need to carry them out.

Set a pace and stick with it

Progress your eFx plan steadily. Develop a plan for every two weeks and be determined to stick with it. This means writing down what you are doing and how many sets of repetitions you do. Even if you feel fabulous on some days be careful not to overdo it - stay within the set limits. Think of the big picture: you'll have good and bad days with your pain, but with slow and steady progress you'll win the race.

Managing food to assist your waist line

When you have LBP that limits your ability to move, shop, prepare food and cook, you have to be highly organised and use food to help you to lose weight. The Rescue Me Flavour Diet is progressive in nature, teaching cooking, tasting, flavouring and portion skills at a pace that will parallel a well structured eFx program.

As you shape a new physical self with the eFx program, the same principles of learning will shape your cooking for a trimmer waist line. For people with chronic LBP, reducing excessive weight will help unload the spine and improve its ability to move. This has to be a great result!

When you have limited standing or walking ability, being prepared with your shopping and cooking is essential. Simple things like a shopping list for the next day's food requirements will allow you to get in and out of the shop as quickly as possible with minimum physical stress. A shopping list can save you money and also, if you stick to it, will mean you avoid impulse buying of junk food on the way out of the supermarket.

Choose to make the difference

Over-protecting an injured person with chronic LBP can contribute to rather than solve problems of LBP and obesity behaviours. Over-nurturing by a partner, siblings, children or friends prevents the affected person taking responsibility for the problem. The key to solving obesity and chronic LBP is choosing to make the difference and then implementing the choice. If someone takes this responsibility away from you, the freedom that you could achieve by making such a choice may never be realised.

Obesity and chronic pain can conspire together to affect your ability to move, value yourself and interact with others. They can also be loud signals suggesting it is time for a change. Listen to this signal and work with your Rescue Me team of family, friends, doctors, therapists and colleagues to make a change which will make a real difference. It's your choice.

Rheumatoid arthritis

Rheumatoid arthritis (RA) is a chronic inflammatory autoimmune disease. The exact causes are unclear, but these factors may increase your risk:

Inheriting specific genes that may make you more susceptible to rheumatoid arthritis.

Being exposed to an infection, possibly a virus or bacterium, that may trigger rheumatoid arthritis in those with an inherited susceptibility.

Being female.

Getting older, because incidence of rheumatoid arthritis increases with age. However, incidence begins to decline in women after menopause

Smoking cigarettes over a long period of time.

The inflammation often affects the joint lining causing pain and swelling and if not medically managed, in severe cases can lead to joint damage, deformity and severe muscle wasting. The disease often goes through periods of remission and then exacerbation. It affects various joints at different times, giving it the characteristics of a roaming disease.

25/five – Matthew, Judith and rheumatoid arthritis

Judith Kennedy was diagnosed with RA when it manifested as a small swelling in her knee 20 years ago. The diagnosis was long in coming, despite multiple trials with various anti-inflammatory drugs aided by management from a high level rheumatologist.

Multiple swellings mainly in the knees, ankles and wrists continued for several years, and resulted in knee, wrist and foot surgery. A deep vein thrombosis (DVT) followed a foot reconstruction which slowed her recovery period and the wrist surgery failed. Extremely severe hip spasms were treated with hospitalisation, morphine and bed rest. Regular flares in wrists and shoulders continued through the next decade with several incidents of hospitalisation as the inflammation continued to roam from one joint to another.

The weight slowly crept on as Judith's professional life in the wine industry continued despite pain and physical inactivity. She had no exercise program and eating too much gourmet food was part of her lifestyle. Frequent severe neck spasms became a major concern with what seemed like no treatment solution. To ease the painful spasms she would have to firmly support her neck with her hands. Her biggest fear was that one day she'd find herself in a retirement home unable to effectively hold her neck or to communicate with people that she was in severe pain.

At this point the treatment was purely medical, through high doses of anti-inflammatory drugs and additional medication for blood pressure that sky rocketed as high as 180/95. Judith's weight reached 202lbs/92kg, with a BMI of 35.5. Despite the severity of the symptoms it was never suggested that weight loss and exercise should form part of the treatment. "It was simply a handful of tablets each day." Then suddenly life changed.

During an accidental meeting with physiotherapist Matthew Squires at an organic fruit market one day, the conversation led to physiotherapy and Pilates management. One week later Judith began her physical rehabilitation journey in

Matthew's clinic. Her goal was to lose 25kg in five months and to solve her neck pain.

Judith's treatment started with hands on. Matthew also had to break it to her that exercise was required to help solve her near-shocking posture. Her head was often rotated to the right and her spine seemed to be holding itself at a point of near exhaustion. Judith was not happy with the state of her body. She wanted a change and she had the motivation to make it happen.

From here it was a bit of a juggling act, balancing pain and Judith's range of available movement to improve her strength. Matthew prescribed pool walking immediately and over time Pilates, and then Gyrotonic were incorporated in her exercise program.

Not everything worked. Judith often wanted a quick result and would jump into some exercises excessively. With a change in her posture she went through months of LBP, which was a relatively new experience. Some exercises were added and subtracted, and still are, to find ways to keep her moving.

During this period Judith and Matthew often discussed food management skills. This was one of Judith's natural strengths. Peaches poached in orange juice and fresh lemon tea became the regular breakfast after pool sessions. Bread was left off the shopping list and low fat milk became the norm. Most importantly, portion control became a motto. Accountability was make or break for her. She was telling everyone - including her publisher - that she wanted to lose weight, get fit and look and feel younger. She had lost only 22lbs/10 kg when she asked Matthew to collaborate on a book which would be the ultimate test of accountability. Because she wanted to lose weight and keep it off. Keep it off. Keep it off.

Today Judith has achieved her target weight at 145lbs/66kg, with a BMI of 23.4. She exercises six days a week, four of them in the pool, and she has just commenced a gym program. She is standing with a straight back and is relatively pain-free. The neck spasms have disappeared and her anti-inflammatory medication dose has been slightly reduced.

For the grandmother of 10 the journey continues as she develops an understanding of her condition and how a team approach to health, food and exercise management is necessary for life, even at the risk of missing a tight deadline for an important book. More importantly Judith maintains her determination even through the low and painful periods of her program. Managing chronic pain for each individual can all too easily become clouded and lost during a painful exacerbation. However her 'eye on the bigger picture' of long term health management allows a physiotherapist such as Matthew to really help her.

Judith's motto is borrowed from her mother: without health you have nothing.

Chapter 10

The recipe for keeping it off

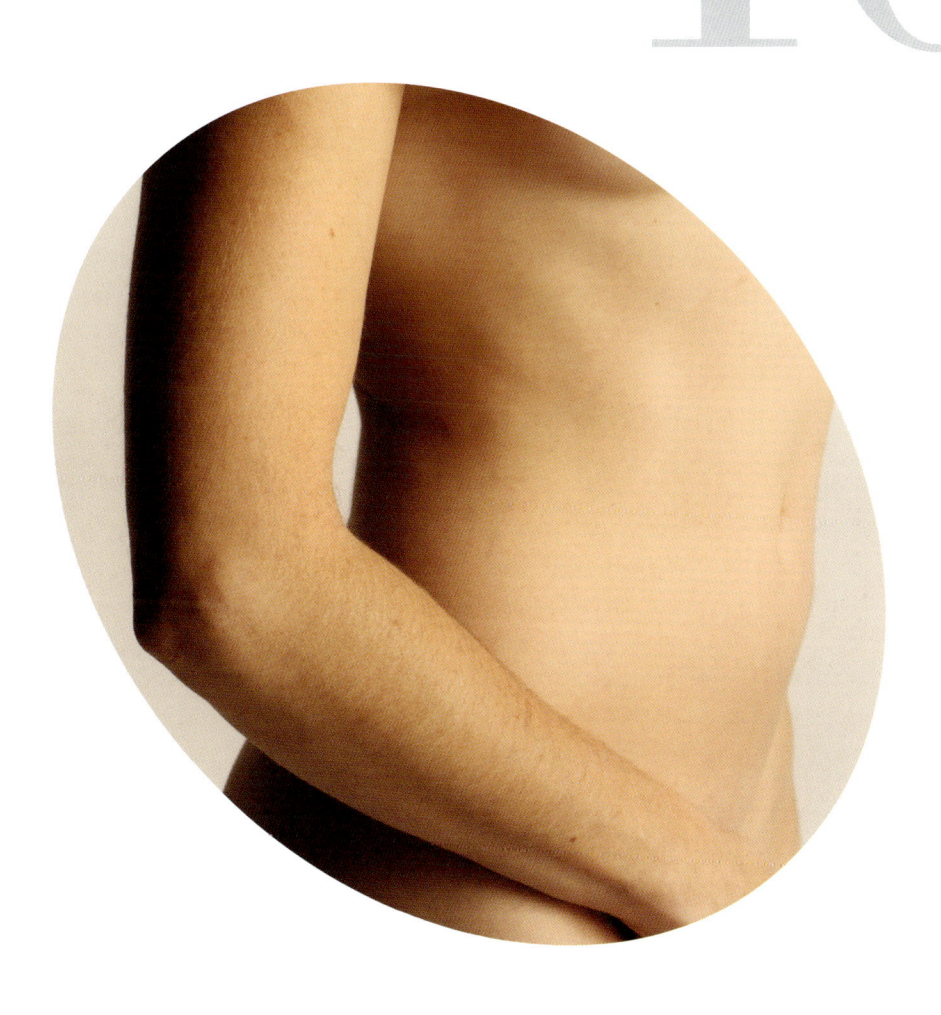

Chapter 10: The recipe for keeping it off

In order to be successful for the long run you need to wake up each day and be prepared to scare yourself for a minute or two by confronting the hard choices you need to make for a lasting, healthier difference. A little bit of fear will drive you to become a Rescue Me graduate.

The reward for sticking to the Rescue Me eFx program and Flavour Diet can be weight loss. However, the real measure of success is better health, increased physical ability and improved cooking skills. Add to this the discovery of free movement and increased flavour in food as new experiences for the full reward.

In chapter 1 we met Bob and Betty Living-Stone, who were facing a choice between moving to the left or the right. To the left represents a step in the direction of greater obesity and the illnesses that come with it. Stepping to the right takes them towards a healthier and fitter life. Regardless of your condition, you have an opportunity to develop a plan – to ignore the step to the left, step to the right and make a lasting change to lose weight and keep it off.

So which way are you choosing to move?

The Rescue Me eFx program is more than a set of exercises for weight loss. It is for anyone - because whether you are overweight or not, you can still become a skilled mover.

Losing weight is a process that moves beyond the concept of repetitive and one-dimensional training, such as sweating it out on an exercise bike or treadmill week in and week out. That method is a sure way to boredom and to becoming an exercise drop-out. To keep you coming back for more, your exercise program has to be interesting, enjoyable, challenging and give you a sense of achievement. These are the factors that get you out of bed on cold winter mornings to brave the rain, or manage the sticky discomfort of the heat in summer.

The eFx reward is the awareness of the progression to exciting, more skilled, full body movements that keep you feeling and looking healthier for longer. Pilates, Gyrokinesis methodology, aquacise and gym are all good cross-training methods to kick start your body. But the real success is when your body uses its newfound strength and co-ordination to maintain its everyday sense of wellbeing. A body that sits easier, moves more freely, breathes more deeply, and beats to a healthier rhythm is worth striving for. You don't have to limit yourself to the exercises described in the eFx program.

With different exercise styles use the five Es to help get the best weight loss effect. Always progress at the right pace, based on your skill level, and set achievable goals for the long-term.

The Rescue Me Flavour Diet allows you to develop the right food choices over and over again, and to incorporate these into the way you prepare, cook and value your food each day. Fresh and creative cooking is worth the effort, and when carried out thoughtfully will complement your eFx program. It can be quicker than it looks if you use some of the tips in the Flavour Diet and maintain the opportunity for success with a well-stocked pantry and by continually replenishing your fresh ingredients.

The Flavour Diet is more than a 12-week weight loss plan. It is more results-based and exciting than that! It provides you with the opportunity to stop and re-evaluate your concepts of food and cooking. Flavour is a full experience that travels beyond the taste buds. It is an ongoing lifestyle choice. It's also the stories around the dinner table, picnics in the park, breakfast on the veranda and the power of good cooking that makes the whole experience more exciting and a more valued part of your rescue plan. If you increase and enhance the flavour of the food you eat, you will manage portion control more efficiently.

Long-term success can start in the kitchen. But it also depends on your imagination, incentives and a few risks when sharing your food experiences with friends or family. You know you are making the right food choices when you discuss one of your own meal combinations, incorporating flavour elements outlined in this book, with a sense of pride. When you are losing weight and improving your cooking skills your success may still wax and wane. If so, go back to the security of the Flavour Diet and pick a favourite week or two to repeat.

At any point pick the book up and re-read it because you will always find a gem or two of advice that may make the difference.

The decision to change

There is a critical moment in every person's life when they realise that it's time to lose weight. Recognising that moment is vital to maintaining your determination and intention to lose the weight for the long-term,

Some people recognise that they need to change either for image or health reasons (and often both), but feel that they have to do a little work on themselves before they can go to the gym and feel comfortable exercising in front of others. Some people will start an exercise weight loss program in secret, early in the morning or late at night, with layers of clothes on out on the footpath. Hopefully they quickly reach the point where they feel comfortable walking into the gym. Some never get that far because they hold tightly onto the problem of weight loss and are too embarrassed to share it with others in case of failure.

What's important is making the choice, even if the benefits take a while to come into effect. If you want to be rescued and experience success, you have to be visible to be saved. You have to make the choice.

The recipe for keeping it off

Establish your weight loss and health improvement goals.

Write your plan down in a format that allows you to add food and exercise elements as you go. Include your BMI and any other important health information.

Photocopy pages from the Flavour Diet and stick them on your fridge. Stick them next to your eFx program and up date them both regularly.

Tell your friends and family what your goal is - this will keep you committed.

Take your clothes off and stand in front of the mirror for self evaluation.

Weigh yourself every day - this will remind you of your goals.

Measure your waist line every two weeks.

Tell your friends once or twice more what your goal is - it helps.

Read this book again to understand the Flavour Diet and decide on the choices for your own exercise program. Know where to start and how to progress by using the forms in chapter 3.

Work initially with a doctor or physical therapist and get going with confidence. Keep in touch with them and consult them on a regular basis.

Now that you have made the decision, keep focused. Get excited about it.

Adopt the Rescue Me Flavour Diet and work hard on portion control.

Have a go at making your own mind map as described in chapter 2. The maps may seem a little unusual at first, but they are an important element of defining the problem you have to manage. Don't underestimate them and repeat them over time.

Re-evaluate your program on a regular basis and discuss it with family or friends.

Troubleshoot the plans to fit into your life and the lives of those around you.

Recognise that your weight loss program will not be static and will be forever changing.

Write at the top of your plan in large type I HAVE MADE THE CHOICE.

Your choice

Now look in the mirror and see yourself as a person moving with determination. You are in charge of your own rescue.

Understanding yourself is the secret. Knowing how much of the Rescue Me concept you need to integrate into your life is the answer.

CHAPTER 10 | THE RECIPE FOR KEEPING IT OFF 185

Peter Mac,
Cuisine Consultant

ACKNOWLEDGEMENTS

RESCUE ME EXECUTIVE CHEF
Peter Mac, Cuisine Consultant, Sydney

PROFESSIONAL ADVISORS
Professor Peter Gunning, Chair Oncology Research Unit, Children's Hospital Westmead
Professor Ian Caterson, Head of Nutrition, University of Sydney
Dr Roger Adams, Senior Lecturer Physiotherapy, University of Sydney
Dr Max Lake OAM. Surgeon, Winemaker, Wine and Food Judge, Author, Friend and Advisor
Dr Louise Dolan MSc. MBBS [Hons]. M PsychMed
Ross Lewis, CEO, Oncology Children's Foundation

FAMILY
Kate, Paul, Cassie, Lexe and Henry Meyer. Daniel Wells. Colette Squires.

READERS
Robin Barnes (Dietician), Cheryl Brownlow (Dietician), Malene Bhargava (Physiotherapist),
Dr Nada Hamad, Hon Wendy Fatin, Hon Dr Sally Talbot MLC, Beth Prindiville, Paul Meyer,
Madeleine Kearney, Andrea Thompson, Elsie Rowles, Eileen Howat, Allan Kearney, Helen Grant.

CHAPTER 4
Amanda Jarman (Gyrotonic and Pilates Instructor)
Mori Traoré (African dancer and teacher)

Cast: David Wong, John Selby, Ann Kearney, Judith Shuttleworth, Julie Hogan, Eileen Howat, Megan Winch, Rachael Bangoura, Angela Perry, David Pidcock, Dedrie O'Rourke, Kate, Paul, Cassie, Lexe and Henry Meyer. Tom and Jake Prindiville.

Gyrotonic Sales Corporation

WINE AND FOOD CONTRIBUTORS
Mike Dobrovic, Mulderbosh Winery, South Africa
Dalene Kukn, Flagstone Winery, South Africa
James Healy, Dog Point Winery, New Zealand
Darren Ho, Hunter Valley Executive Chef

SPECIAL THANKS FOR THE FOLLOWING LOCATIONS:
Newington College, Stanmore, Sydney (pool and gyms)
Universal Motion Physiotherapy Studio, Stanmore, Sydney (pages 71, 78 and 79)
Chef Peter Mac (test kitchen)

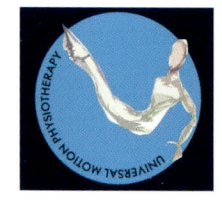

REFERENCES

Aldo Ferrara L. Guida L. Ferrara F. De Luca G. Castaldo R. Viola S. Russo R. Blood pressure at rest, during 24 h monitoring and in response to sympathetic stimulation in hypertensive patients with metabolic syndrome. *International Journal of Cardiology*. 117(3):312-6, 2007 May 2.

American College of Sports Medicine: ACSM's resource manual for Guidelines for exercise testing and prescription 5th ed. Editors Kaminsky L, Kimberly B, Garber C, Glass S, Hamm L, Kohl H, and Mikesky A Baltimore: Lippincott Williams & Wilkins, c2006.

Austin SB. Melly SJ. Sanchez BN. Patel A. Buka S. Gortmaker SL. Clustering of fast-food restaurants around schools: a novel application of spatial statistics to the study of food environments. *American Journal of Public Health*. 95(9):1575-81, 2005 Sep.

Budd GM. Hayman LL. Childhood obesity: determinants, prevention, and treatment. *Journal of Cardiovascular Nursing*. 2006 Nov-Dec; 21(6): 437-41.

Caballero AE. Metabolic and vascular abnormalities in subjects at risk for type 2 diabetes: the early start of a dangerous situation. *Archives of Medical Research*. 36(3):241-9, 2005 May-Jun.

Chandalia M. Abate N. Metabolic complications of obesity: inflated or inflamed?. *Journal of Diabetes & its Complications*. 21(2):128-36, 2007 Mar-Apr.

Clement K. Ferre P. Genetics and the pathophysiology of obesity. *Pediatric Research*. 53(5):721-5, 2003 May.

Close RN. Schoeller DA. The financial reality of overeating. *Journal of the American College of Nutrition*. 25(3):203-9, 2006 Jun.

Cole TJ. Freeman JV. Preece MA. Body mass index reference curves for the UK, 1990. *Archives of Disease in Childhood*. 73(1):25-9, 1995 Jul.

Dandona P. Aljada A. Chaudhuri A. Mohanty P. Garg R. Metabolic syndrome: a comprehensive perspective based on interactions between obesity, diabetes, and inflammation. *Circulation*. 111(11):1448-54, 2005 Mar 22.

Daniels SR. Arnett DK. Eckel RH. Gidding SS. Hayman LL. Kumanyika S. Robinson TN. Scott BJ. St Jeor S. Williams CL. Overweight in children and adolescents: pathophysiology, consequences, prevention, and treatment *Circulation*. 111(15):1999-2012, 2005 Apr 19.

Eppens MC. Craig ME. Cusumano J. Hing S. Chan AK. Howard NJ. Silink M. Donaghue KC. Prevalence of diabetes complications in adolescents with type 2 compared with type 1 diabetes. *Diabetes Care*. 29(6):1300-6, 2006 Jun.

Fanuele JC. Abdu WA. Hanscom B. Weinstein JN. Association between obesity and functional status in patients with spine disease. *Spine*. 27(3):306-12, 2002 Feb 1.

Gidding SS. Dennison BA. Birch LL. Daniels SR. Gillman MW. Gilman MW. Lichtenstein AH. Rattay KT. Steinberger J. Stettler N. Van Horn L. Dietary recommendations for children and adolescents: a guide for practitioners: consensus statement from the American Heart Association. *Circulation*. 2005 Sep 27; 112(13): 2061-75.

Griffin TM. Guilak F. The role of mechanical loading in the onset and progression of osteoarthritis. *Exercise & Sport Sciences Reviews*. 33(4):195-200, 2005 Oct.

Hanley AJ. Karter AJ. Williams K. Festa A. D'Agostino RB Jr. Wagenknecht LE. Haffner SM. Prediction of type 2 diabetes mellitus with alternative definitions of the metabolic syndrome: the Insulin Resistance Atherosclerosis Study. *Circulation*. 112(24):3713-21, 2005 Dec 13.

Kouba M Quality of organic animal products. *Livestock Production Science*. 80(1-2) 33-40, 2003 Mar.

Lake JK. Power C. Cole TJ. Back pain and obesity in the 1958 British birth cohort. cause or effect?. *Journal of Clinical Epidemiology*. 53(3):245-50, 2000 Mar 1.

Laurey R Simkin-Silverman Rena R Wing Menopause *Postgraduate Medicine* Vol 108 No3, 2000 Sept.

Levine AA. Excessive fruit juice consumption: how can something that causes failure to thrive be associated with obesity? *Journal of Pediatric Gastroenterology & Nutrition*. 25(5):554-5, 1997 Nov.

Libby P. Fat fuels the flame: triglyceride-rich lipoproteins and arterial inflammation. *Circulation Research*. 100(3):299-301, 2007 Feb 16.

Lin KC. Tsai ST. Kuo SC. Tsay SL. Chou P. Interrelationship between insulin resistance and menopause on the metabolic syndrome and its individual component among nondiabetic women in the kinmen study. American *Journal of the Medical Sciences*. 333(4):208-14, 2007 Apr.

Lockie S. Lyons K. Lawrence G. Grice J. Choosing organics: a path analysis of factors underlying the selection of organic food among Australian consumers. *Appetite*. 43(2):135-46, 2004 Oct.

Loney P and Stratford The prevalence of low back pain in adults: a methodological review of the literature. *Physical Therapy* 79:384-396, 1999.

Magill R: Motor learning and control : concepts and applications 8th ed. Boston: McGraw-Hill, c2007.

McCallum Z. Wake M. Gerner B. Harris C. Gibbons K. Gunn J. Waters E. Baur LA. Can Australian general practitioners tackle childhood overweight/obesity? Methods and processes from the LEAP (Live, Eat and Play) randomised controlled trial. *Journal of Paediatrics & Child Health*. 41(9-10):488-94, 2005 Sep-Oct.

Menezes A Pilates – The Complete Works By Joseph H. Pilates. Your Health and Return to Life Through Contrology. Australia: Pilates Institute of Australasia 2002.

Mesch VR. Boero LE. Siseles NO. Royer M. Prada M. Sayegh F. Schreier L. Benencia HJ. Berg GA. Metabolic syndrome throughout the menopausal transition: influence of age and menopausal status. *Climacteric*. 9(1):40-8, 2006 Feb.

Mule G. Nardi E. Cottone S. Cusimano P. Incalcaterra F. Palermo A. Giandalia ME. Mezzatesta G. Andronico G. Cerasola G. Relationship of metabolic syndrome with pulse pressure in patients with essential hypertension. *American Journal of Hypertension*. 20(2):197-203, 2007 Feb.

Petter LP. Hourihane JO. Rolles CJ. Is water out of vogue? A survey of the drinking habits of 2-7 year olds. *Archives of Disease in Childhood*. 72(2):137-40, 1995 Feb.

Simkin-Silverman LR. Wing RR. Boraz MA. Kuller LH. Lifestyle intervention can prevent weight gain during menopause: Results from a 5-year randomized clinical trial. *Annals of Behavioral Medicine*. 26(3) 212-220, 2003 Dec.

Sothern MS. Obesity prevention in children: physical activity and nutrition. *Nutrition*. 2004 Jul-Aug; 20(7/8): 704-8.

St-Onge MP. Keller KL. Heymsfield SB. Changes in childhood food consumption patterns: a cause for concern in light of increasing body weights. *American Journal of Clinical Nutrition*. 78(6):1068-73, 2003 Dec.

The Definition of Obese USA. *The Guardian* 4 June 2005

Townsend MS. Peerson J. Love B. Achterberg C. Murphy SP. Food insecurity is positively related to overweight in women. *Journal of Nutrition*. 131(6):1738-45, 2001 Jun.

Waddell G A new clinical model for the treatment of low-back pain. *Spine* 1987 Sep;12(7):632-44.

Waddell G The Back Pain Revolution. United Kingdom: Churchill Livingstone 1998.

Wardlow G: Perspectives in nutrition 7th ed. Boston: McGraw-Hill Higher Education, c2007.

Westerterp-Plantenga MS. Verwegen CR. Ijedema MJ. Wijckmans NE. Saris WH. Acute effects of exercise or sauna on appetite in obese and nonobese men. *Physiology & Behavior*. 62(6):1345-54, 1997 Dec.

www.abs.gov.au (Australian Bureau of Statistics) Cardiovascular disease in Australia: A snapshot, 2004-2005

www.asso.org.au (Australasian Society for the Study of Obesity) Obesity in Australian Children

Yang WS. Chuang LM. Human genetics of adiponectin in the metabolic syndrome. *Journal of Molecular Medicine*. 84(2):112-21, 2006 Feb.

We would like to acknowledge our thanks to all the authors and societies of references, articles, books, journals and web sites that we referenced while writing this book and realise that some references may have been missed in our acknowledgement in the final composition.